1987

American Formalism and the Problem of Interpretation

J. Timothy Bagwell is professor of German and Comparative
Literature at the University of California, Riverside

American Formalism and the Problem of Interpretation

J. Timothy Bagwell

Rice University Press   Houston, Texas

First Edition, 1986

Requests for permission to reproduce material
from this work should be addressed to:

Rice University Press

Rice University

Post Office Box 1892

Houston, Texas 77251

Library of Congress Cataloging-in-Publication Data

Bagwell, J. Timothy (James Timothy), 1952–

    American formalism and the problem of interpretation.

    Bibliography: p. 125

    1. New Criticism—United States—Addresses, essays,
lectures. I. Title.

PN98.N4B34   1986   801′.95′0973   85–30096

ISBN 0–89263–260–7

Library of Congress Catalog Card Number 85-30096

ISBN 0–89263–260–7

For my mother and father

I am not the I who writes,
but the eye is ours which parts the fire
in things unseen and then, seen.

—*Philip Lamantia*

ACKNOWLEDGMENTS

This book would not have been possible without
the help and encouragement of my teachers,
Paul Hernadi, Wolfgang Iser, and Rudolf Kuenzli.

CONTENTS

AUTHOR'S FOREWORD
xi

INTRODUCTION
1

CHAPTER 1
Wimsatt and Beardsley
and the Problem of the
Intentional Fallacy
5

CHAPTER 2
Validity in Authority:
E. D. Hirsch
29

CHAPTER 3
Stanley Fish:
The Reader as Author
65

CHAPTER 4
When Literature Is:
Dual Meaning Versus
Equivalent Meaning
89

NOTES
105

GLOSSARY
119

BIBLIOGRAPHY
125

AUTHOR'S FOREWORD

Since the completion of this book, I have had the benefit of several vigorous readings. Many of the criticisms I have received have helped me to put the manuscript into its present form; others, alas, address problems that remain to be solved. Without denying the importance or the validity of this second category, I would like to offer a couple of reasons for what might seem to be a major oversight: the absence of discussion of recent developments in critical theory on the Continent.

Since structuralism and post-structuralism have supplanted New Criticism in this country, it seemed to me rather anticlimactic to look at New Criticism (or American formalism, as we now prefer to call it) in the light of structuralist and post-structuralist aesthetics. Structuralism does not clarify the debate concerning the "intentional fallacy"—it denies it in denying the integrity of both authorial intention and the "text itself." The total absence of the debate in current literary-theoretical discussion is testimony to the thoroughness with which the ground has been covered and New Criticism laid to rest in it.

What concerned me in undertaking this project was not only the need to take the debate in America on its own terms, but also the belief that the debate had not been properly understood, even by those taking part in it. This misunderstanding was due in my opinion precisely to a misunderstanding of the notion of (authorial) intention as something distinct from textuality and a concomitant reification of the "text" as something independent of consciousness. However, clarifying these concepts (as opposed to dispensing with them) seemed a worthwhile task, especially if one considers what hangs in the balance: the existence and nature of literary discourse. Indeed, that is what the "intentional fallacy" argument is all about (not about whether to read biography or whether a poem is really a thing), and that fact, if only for historical reasons, is worth knowing.

However, my exclusion of any detailed discussion of post-Husserlian developments on the Continent does invite two legitimate criticisms. First, Husserl's theory of subjectivity has come under heavy attack by

later phenomenologists (notably Heidegger and Gadamer), structuralists, and post-structuralists (notably Derrida). Second, it is precisely
these critics of Husserl—so it might seem—that underlie the work of
Stanley Fish; it is unfair, therefore, to fault Fish for failing to be
Husserlian.

There is no question but that a phenomenological theory of literary
discourse, such as the one I begin to develop here, must be situated
within the debates between phenomenology and existential phenomenology, structuralism, and post-structuralism, respectively. The
question was whether to write a longer book or another book. I chose
the latter alternative, a sequel, and in it I deal with the problems raised
in these debates. The reason for my choice was in part, as I mentioned
earlier, the desire to offer a self-contained historical account of a problem in American hermeneutics.

However, I wrote the present book with the existential phenomenologists Maurice Merleau-Ponty, Paul Ricoeur, and Hans-Georg Gadamer
firmly in mind, and I am perhaps guilty of reading Husserl too much in
their light. In any case, the relevant criticisms of Husserl can be reduced
to three major points, all of which are compatible with my position on
the hermeneutic problem of intention. Husserl's critics understand the
intending subject increasingly (1) as contingent upon or as a back-
formation of intentionality (for Sartre and Merleau-Ponty, perception;
for Merleau-Ponty, Ricoeur, and the structuralists, language; for
Heidegger and Gadamer, history and language; for Derrida, writing),
(2) as existential, that is, caught up in the experience of being as opposed
to being accessible as an object of knowledge, and (3) predetermined by
the very alienated and alienating "natural attitude" that Husserl imagines so easily set aside.

Objection (1) is precisely what grounds the *Wirkungsästhetik* (reader-
response theory) of Wolfgang Iser, a student of Gadamer's. Iser's
theory I consider to be a defensible—if not yet entirely defended—
account of how the reader is constituted as subject by the text in an
"effective history" (*Wirkungsgeschichte*). (1) is furthermore the basis of
the parallel (rather than opposing) alignment of author and reader vis
à vis the text that I discuss (chapter one), and the accompanying necessary recognition that the hermeneutics of intention is logically prior to
what we reify as author, reader, *or* text. In this regard, I accept
Gadamer's and Iser's conception of understanding as a "fusion of
horizons" (*Horizontsverschmelzung*).

Objection (2) is the basis of my distinction between literary and nonliterary discourse (or rather approaches to/functions of discourse), a distinction that is developed more fully in the next book. But it is worth noting here that, even though Husserl's distinction between intentionality and the natural attitude (the basis of the theory developed in this book) has come under heavy attack (especially from Heidegger and Derrida), some version of the distinction in (2), and hence of Husserl's distinction, is never absent from the attack, least of all in Heidegger and Derrida. Deconstruction presupposes that which is as yet undeconstructed.

I have become increasingly troubled by objection (3) as I have come to realize more and more the close interdependence of the *subtilitas intelligendi* and the *subtilitas explicandi* (chapter two). The implication of this for literary criticism is simply that the understanding of literary meaning may be determined by what my old poetry-writing instructor called the DHM (deep hidden meaning, paraphrased) rather than the other way around. In fact, this possibility is raised early on in this book as one position in the debate around authorial intention (p. 16, IIIb), and again in my conclusion (p. 102). My point is that, even if something like the natural attitude determines something like intentionality, that does not necessarily mean that they are the same thing. An illustration that comes to mind is the famous "duck-rabbit" that the gestalt psychologists are fond of citing. The question that interests me is not so much whether I see a duck or a rabbit because the ambiguous drawing has been identified for me in advance as a duck or a rabbit, but whether in the words of Wittgenstein it is "like something" to see a duck *or* a rabbit in the drawing, and whether that experience is different in any important way from the other one or from the referential designation provided by the label.

As for Stanley Fish, I think it is debatable whether he is to be counted among the post-phenomenologists (to coin what seems to me a useful term) like Heidegger and Derrida. The point of my chapter on Fish is precisely that he is that side, not this side, of Husserl. The subject Fish criticizes is that of Descartes, the same one attacked by Husserl himself. Fish hardly gets beyond Husserl's First Cartesian Meditation before casting himself from the pinnacle of skepticism confident that he will be saved by the angels of relativism. Husserl, on the other hand, especially in the Fifth Meditation, develops a notion of the subject's contingency and otherness that anticipates in some ways Lacan and Derrida.

One final note: Wimsatt's *The Verbal Icon* was published in 1954, but the essay "The Intentional Fallacy" (chapter one) appeared eight years earlier in the *Sewanee Review* (LIV, Summer, 1946). Wimsatt and Beardsley's essay appeared in an earlier form as an article entitled "Intention" in *Dictionary of World Literature,* Joseph T. Shipley, ed. (1942). There are certainly other precursors of Wimsatt and Beardsley's theory—they cite even Plato's Socrates in support thereof—but recently I came across the following very explicit formulation, which predates Wimsatt and Beardsley's by seven years, in the writings of the French philosopher Emile Chartier Alain (a contemporary of Paul Valéry):

> If I were to write about art, I would stress that it is a kind of doing rather than a kind of thinking. This characteristic is the most noticeable, and yet is almost completely forgotten. For usually one discusses the plan of a work and considers what the artist intended, in order to compare it with what he has realized. Certainly there is no work without a scheme; but that in the work that is work of art depends solely upon the execution and appears to the artist only during the execution.*

This last notion is only hinted at in Wimsatt and Beardsley, but it is squarely in the philosophical tradition of Croce and Cassirer (as well as Gadamer), and it anticipates many of the problems dealt with in this book as well (I hope) as some of the objections to the way they are dealt with.

---

* "Doing as Source of the Beautiful" (November 15, 1935, my translation), reprinted in *Akzente,* 31:2 (April 1984), p. 143.

INTRODUCTION

For years now, critics have discussed the problem of authorial intention in literary interpretation as if the concept of "intention" were something that could be taken for granted. Yet, according to the *Encyclopedia of Philosophy,*

> the word "intention" is ambiguous in the way . . . that the word "belief" is ambiguous, for . . . the word may refer either to a state or episode (in this case intending) or to the intentional object of such a state or episode—that is, to that which is intended.[1]

It is fairly obvious that the debate about "authorial intention" is fueled by this ambiguity: W. K. Wimsatt and Monroe C. Beardsley are able to argue the notion of the "intentional fallacy" because they are able to argue a distinction between the author's intention as "episode" and the literary "object"; E. D. Hirsch and Peter D. Juhl, on the other hand, presuppose that intention *is* the literary object, and hence are able to argue the legitimacy of adducing intentional evidence. It is also clear that the term "meaning" (which Wimsatt and Beardsley distinguish from "intention") is ambiguous in the same way. Consider the following sentences:

A. 1) Did you intend for us to laugh at your remark?

2) Did you mean for us to laugh at your remark?

B. 1) What did you intend by that remark?

2) What did you mean by that remark?

These sentences seem to indicate that the actions corresponding to the terms "meaning" and "intention" may be more or less identical. The debate about authorial intention can thus be understood as a debate about the nature of meaning, especially literary meaning; at the same

1

time, the concept of meaning may well be illuminated by a clarification
of the concept of intention. Ambiguity is suggested in the etymology of
the word "intention" itself, which derives from Latin roots meaning to
"stretch out or forth" or to "direct" (*The Oxford English Dictionary*).
"Intention" implies a metaphorical motion between two points of poles,
more specifically, between a subject and an object. When the first pole
(the subject) is identified with the "intention," we get a view of intention
as distinct from the intentional object (in the case of literature,
"meaning"). When the second pole (the object) is identified with
"intention," we get a view of intention *as* meaning.

The most obvious manifestation of the inherent ambiguity of the
term "intention" is to be found in the distinction between intention as
plan and intention as *accomplishment*. Wimsatt and Beardsley insist that
the plan of an author is not an adequate standard for measuring the
success of his or her work. However, this is not generally the point of
contention for their critics. It is not so much the distinction between the
plan to mean something and meaning itself which critics like Hirsch and
Juhl challenge as that between the accomplished meaning of the author
and that of the text.

Because the real issue is indeed the distinction (or lack of one) between author's meaning and textual meaning, the debate about
"authorial intention" is a debate about the possibility and nature of
communication and (since, at least with regard to literature, most of us
are readers rather than writers) interpretation. Communication and
interpretation are in turn two sides of a single question, that of the
sharability of cognition.

Obviously, the outcome of the debate about authorial intention will
affect larger issues such as the nature of literature, the function of
criticism, and the possibility of validity in interpretation. In fact, as I try
to show in chapter one, the concept of the "intentional fallacy" is tied up
with a concept of literary discourse as distinct from nonliterary discourse. The debate about "authorial intention" can thus be seen as a
debate about whether or not there is a uniquely "literary" form of
expression. Wimsatt and Beardsley seem to have as their major goal the
preservation of literary meaning. "The Intentional Fallacy" (1946) can
be viewed in retrospect as a veritable manifesto of American formalism.
For it only makes sense to dismiss intentionalist arguments from literary
discussion if a case can be made for the existence and priority of the *text
itself*. Inevitably (given Wimsatt's own preoccupation with "style") the
New Criticism came to be associated with an interest in purely formal

rather than semantic elements of literary language, that is, with stylistics. Since meaning can be expressed in different ways (as authorial statements of intention, by their very existence, attest), the only stable entities peculiar to a particular utterance such as that of a poem would seem to be things such as rhyme, rhythm, diction, syntax, or at best figurative language understood as mere decoration.

Whether right or wrong, such a view of "formalism" seems to underlie the intense criticism that the New Critics have provoked, especially in recent years. In this book I would like to propose a *semantic* understanding of the notion of the intentional fallacy and the formalism it aims at; in other words, I will attempt to defend the notion of what Hirsch calls "semantic autonomy" by showing how it is not the contradiction in terms it seems to be.

Hirsch, reacting to the greater freedom accorded by the New Criticism to the activity of literary interpretation, insists that literature does not mean differently from linguistic utterances in general, and he does so precisely in order to preserve what he conceives to be literature's meaning. More recently, however, Hirsch has had to yield some of his claims regarding the author to meet what he perceives as an attack on meaning and interpretation from still other critics of Wimsatt and Beardsley, critics who deny that literature is distinct from "ordinary" discourse because, for them, all discourse is fictive, or figurative, or subject to the vagaries of interpretation.

If, as a recent article in *The Chronicle of Higher Education* suggests, "the 'moldy fig academics' are lining up against the 'hermeneutical mafia' in literature departments across the country,"[2] it might be that a clarification of the notion of "intention" (and its implications for the concept of "literature") will play a role in deciding one of the most crucial critical questions of our time. My test case is the theory of Stanley Fish, not only because he comes to the "hermeneutical mafia" by way of an admittedly New Critical approach to literature (affective stylistics), but also because he is one of the most formidable and vocal proponents of the notion that the problem of intention is not a real problem at all. According to Fish, both the Wimsatt/Beardsley camp and the Hirsch camp are wrong, because neither the text *nor* the author exists independently of the act of interpretation.

In chapter four, I attempt to vindicate the doctrine of the "intentional fallacy" (in the broader form of the "interpretive fallacy") by demonstrating how the notion of literary discourse can be grounded philosophically in terms of the concept of intentionality itself. What we might call a literary *function* or *use* of language is a systematic reduction of the nonintentional (referential) mode that characterizes practical discourse to the level of intention—of cognition of meaning—itself. Such a vindication will, I hope, transcend the conflict between two sides for both of which (moldy fig and mafioso alike) the concept of literature seems to be no longer viable.

Because each chapter serves a slightly different purpose, there are slight differences in format between them. Chapter one is concerned with a general statement of the problem of the "intentional fallacy" (and its relation to literary discourse and interpretation) and with the general outlines of the debate that problem engendered. Chapter two concerns a specific position within that debate, one which has received a great deal of attention and which presents the greatest challenge to Wimsatt and Beardsley's original theory. Chapter three concerns a theory that is only tangentially related to the problem of intention, but whose implications for that problem are profound. Consequently, in chapter one most of the secondary sources have been incorporated into the text as part of the history of the debate. In chapter two, more of the discussion from secondary sources has been relegated to the footnotes, since the purpose of the chapter is less to outline the dimensions and history of a critical problem than to analyze a single position taken with regard to that problem. This is even more true of chapter three, where I did not want to get too bogged down in all of the problems—there are many— for which Fish's theory has implications, but wanted rather to stick to what in his theory is relevant to the problem of intention.

1

Wimsatt and Beardsley and the Problem of the Intentional Fallacy

The Intentional Fallacy and Literary Meaning

In "The Intentional Fallacy," five axiomatic propositions are set forth in support of the assertion that "the design or intention of the author is neither available nor desirable as a standard for judging the success of a work of literary art."[1] I am paraphrasing:

1. A poem is the creation of an author. But the fact that the author is the "cause" of the poem does not mean that he or she is the "standard" for its evaluation.

2. An external statement of the author's intention is irrelevant because, if the intention is manifested in the poem, the statement is superfluous, and if the intention is not manifested in the poem, the statement is to no purpose.

3. A poem must "work." It is only if the poem does work that we bother with the intention. "A poem should not mean but be."[2]

4. It is true that a poem "expresses a personality," but it does so in a way that is "dramatic." Therefore, "we ought to impute the thoughts and attitudes of the poem immediately to the dramatic *speaker*, and if to the author at all, only by an act of biographical inference."

5. The poet, by revision, may improve the poem but he or she does not better achieve an original intention; rather, we would say that the poet has achieved a different intention.

5

"He's the man we were in search of, that's true," says Hardy's rustic constable, "and yet he's not the man we were in search of. For the man we were in search of was not the man we wanted" [p. 5].

To the argument that "the poem is not the critic's own," Wimsatt and Beardsley reply: agreed, but neither is it therefore the author's alone. They wish to avoid both of these "forms of irresponsibility." This is the central tenet of their argument, as Wimsatt's juxtaposition of "The Intentional Fallacy" and "The Affective Fallacy" at the beginning of *The Verbal Icon* suggests.

Wimsatt is well aware of the problem involved in maintaining that the text is located in a metaphorical space between author and reader. In his introduction he concedes that

the poem conceived as a thing in between the poet and the audience is of course an abstraction. The poem is an act. The only substantive entities are the poet and the audience [p. xvii].

But if the poem is to yield itself as an object of criticism, argues Wimsatt, it must be "hypostatized."

Wimsatt and Beardsley are primarily concerned with the relation of the dispute over intention to what they see as the central problem of evaluation. Arguing against one intentionalist (Ananda K. Coomaraswamy) who sees the two primary questions of criticism as (1) "whether the artist achieved his intentions," and (2) "whether the work of art 'ought ever to have been undertaken at all,'" Wimsatt and Beardsley make their concerns explicit. Coomaraswamy maintains that the second question leads to *moral* criticism; only the first produces *artistic* criticism. Wimsatt and Beardsley, in preferring the second sort of inquiry, do appeal to "objective criticism of works of art as such," holding (by implication from their earlier arguments) the first sort to be concerned more with the author's plan than his or her execution.[3]

We maintain that (2) is an inquiry of more worth than (1), and since (2) and not (1) is capable of distinguishing poetry from murder [both of which may be "achieved"], the name "artistic criticism" is properly given to (2) [p. 6].

Whereas Wimsatt and Beardsley, both here and elsewhere, emphasize evaluation as the ultimate purpose of "objective criticism," it is not the irrelevance of authorial intention for evaluation which becomes the guiding light of New Criticism and which will later provoke such a hefty reaction from its opponents, but the implied irrelevance of authorial intention for interpretation, as Wimsatt himself will acknowledge.

"An external statement of the author's intention is irrelevant," say Wimsatt and Beardsley. Evidently, what is relevant is what is *internal*. Yet, in discussing the "difference between internal and external evidence for the meaning of a poem," Wimsatt and Beardsley note the ostensible paradox that

> what is . . . internal is also public: it is discovered through the semantics and syntax of a poem, through our habitual knowledge of the language, through grammars, dictionaries, and all the literature which is the source of dictionaries, in general through all that makes a language and culture [p. 10].

This last phrase especially seems to open up the concept of the "poetic text" almost infinitely: it is hard to imagine how "external" evidence, derived from "revelations (in journals . . . or letters or reported conversations) about how or why the poet wrote the poem," would not be included in "all that makes a language and culture." Wimsatt and Beardsley seem to admit as much when they introduce an "intermediate" kind of evidence:

> The meaning of words is the history of words, and the biography of an author, his use of a word, and the associations which the word had for *him*, are part of the word's history and meaning.

At this point, a footnote carries this line of reasoning even further:

> And the history of words [occurring in the poem] *after* a poem is written may contribute meanings which if relevant to the original pattern should not be ruled out by a scruple about intention [p. 281].

Why then should an author's explicit explanations of his uses of words (explanations which are surely a part of those words' histories) be excluded from consideration? Far from blurring the distinction between "internal" and "external" evidence, Wimsatt and Beardsley's emphasis here on the semantic (rather than the purely formal) nature of the "original pattern" makes clear the extent to which the distinction between "internal" and "external" is one between modes of meaning. Clearly, there can be two distinct modes of presentation of the "same" information,[4] one which is "part of the work as a linguistic fact" and one which is not (if only because it is *about* the work).

This point is made clear by a subsequent comment. Speaking of explanatory notes supplied by authors such as T. S. Eliot (for *The Wasteland)* and with "allusiveness" in general (both supposed to be strong arguments for the validity of authorial intention), Wimsatt and Beardsley argue:

> We mean to suggest by the above analysis that whereas notes tend to justify themselves as external indexes to the author's *intention,* yet they ought to be judged like any other parts of a composition . . . , and when so judged their reality as parts of the poem, or their imaginative integration with the rest of the poem, may come into question [p. 16].

The issue raised, then, by the above extension of the notion of what may contribute to the literary meaning of words is not so much the relevance of authorial intention as the distinct nature of literary discourse, which is to a large extent simply assumed in Wimsatt and Beardsley's essay.[5]

One can measure the change and lack of change in focus of Wimsatt's position regarding intention by examining his own summary of the state of the argument in 1968. In "Genesis: A Fallacy Revisited" we see the extent to which his emphasis has shifted from the problem of evaluation to that of interpretation (where the doctrine of the "intentional fallacy" has had the greatest impact):

> It seemed to me then, and it still seems, that Mr. Beardsley and I succeeded in formulating a clear, reasonable, and viable statement of the thesis that the intention of literary artist qua intention is neither a valid ground for arguing *the presence of a quality or a meaning* in a given instance of his literary work nor a valid criterion for judging the value of that work.[6]

The words I have emphasized above indicate a reorientation in Wimsatt's later position, but it is one that is consistent with the way in which the "intentional fallacy" argument had come to be taken in 1968 and, as I see it, with the semantic assumptions underlying Wimsatt and Beardsley's original formulation. Wimsatt is aware of the need for this reorientation:

> The statement in our essay of 1945 should certainly have read: "The design or intention of the author is neither available nor desirable as a standard for judging *either the meaning or the value* of a work of literary art" [p. 221].

(The phrase emphasized replaces "the success.") However, it is also the notion of the "intentional fallacy" that is reflected in this new emphasis that has provoked the most criticism and, indeed, is harder to maintain.

Wimsatt resumes (in both senses) the dialogue about intention with this "new" problem at the center. Among the various sorts of intentionalism he now rejects—(1) historical, biographical; (2) historical, poetic; (3) methodological, explicitly evaluative—we find

> 4. Methodological, interpretive: The character, mind, or habitual meanings of the poet Gray are a valid guide (or the best guide) to the meaning of the *Elegy* [p. 207].

It is this last sort of argument that Wimsatt wants especially to take issue with; in fact, as he warns us, it is a particular subcategory of this argument that disturbs him the most: not the earlier question of the author's expressed intention, but the more general one of what the interpreter knows about the author's life and work.

The first argument Wimsatt addresses (4a in his series) is that intention may be "found in, or inferred from, the work itself" (p. 210). Wimsatt accepts this sort of intentionalism, as he did less directly in 1946. It is unfortunate that many of his and Beardsley's critics (even after 1968) have not read this passage—they might have spared themselves many pains to debunk the doctrine of the "intentional fallacy" on the grounds of just this argument. Later in this essay Wimsatt responds to the alleged "narrowness" of his and Beardsley's concept of intention.

> We took "intention" in a specific or limited sense, because it was just the difference between this sense and the broader (or other) sense that we believed to be often obscured in critical argument [p. 221].

Unfortunately, this is as close as Wimsatt comes to responding to a theory of intention which cuts straight through the above difference, the theory set forth eight years earlier by E. D. Hirsch.

The author's intention has a limited (in no way binding) "advisory" usefulness (argument 4b). Again, Wimsatt accepts this notion, defusing one of the strongest arguments against his theory: that the intention of the author may well guide and even coincide with the interpretation of the poem. We should, however, notice that Wimsatt has yielded some ground, since he no longer insists on the irrelevance of such a guide. His earlier argument (axiom 2, above) served to establish the semantic autonomy of literary discourse; with that notion firmly established, Wimsatt is perhaps now able to allow authorial intention a small role in the establishment of a semantic entity that must nonetheless stand on its own.

Authorial intention may serve to fill in gaps or missing parts of the work (4c). Wimsatt and Beardsley had discussed this problem in 1946 in connection with Eliot's allusiveness in *The Wasteland*. Now, as then, Wimsatt feels that authorial utterances such as Eliot's explanatory notes are best regarded as "loosely attached parts of poems" (p. 211). As such, their necessity—and the same might be argued for the need for the author's "advisory" function—seems to indicate "some deficiency in the work of art itself." The idea that the same authorial utterance could be regarded as either "poem" or "intention" indicates once again the special status that is being attributed, not just to literary discourse, but to the act of *regarding* discourse as literary.

It is not exactly clear what Wimsatt is arguing against in 4d, since he presents only a counter-argument; namely, that

> there are features of gross material or of structure in art works which not only do not call for the artist's intention to help their interpretation but will even strongly defy contrary indications [p. 212].

For example, continues Wimsatt, a granite statue remains granite, even if the author thought he or she was working in marble; a poem in French defies the author's belief that he was writing in English. Less farfetched is the observation (made by Samuel Johnson) that whether or not Shakespeare's violations of the Aristotelian unities were intentional cannot and need not be resolved, because Shakespeare's violations of the unities are undeniably a characteristic of the texts themselves and are to be judged as successful or unsuccessful on their own merits.

Argument 4d seems to serve as a counter-example to 4b. As such, it seems less than conclusive, since even a correct statement of authorial intention must, according to Wimsatt, be kept distinct from the concrete artistic achievement. More important is the fact that the notion of a pure medium (such as granite) is arguably inapplicable to a system of symbols (language) which is mediated by the cognitive act of interpretation. A statue may be made of granite, but a poem is not in any crucial sense made of ink and paper. The fact *that* the words of the poem are French is certainly beyond question, but then such questions regarding the explicit form (or even meaning) of the poem are not generally what we disagree about. In any case, the existence of a purely formal level of meaning in poetry (the central theme of *The Verbal Icon*) is part of the argument being defended and should therefore not be assumed in the defense.

The poet may or may not be the best or most honest interpreter of his or her own work; only the "context" of the poem can help to determine the best interpretation (4e). Like 4d, 4e seems to present an unattached counter-example (Johnson's correction of Goldsmith's interpretation of the latter's own poem). However, this example does not exclude the possibility that the poet might also be right about his work (as one would suspect often to be the case).

For this reason, 4e (though not the argument Wimsatt is most concerned with) raises a crucial question. Up to this point, the argument has centered around the criteria for a valid interpretation. But it seems to me clearly possible that Goldsmith (or, for that matter, Johnson) could provide an interpretation which, even though correct, would nonetheless *not* be the same as the author's. This possibility calls into question the status of interpretive discourse. Interpretation is, by implication, not authoritative (not identical to the achieved meaning of the poem); hence, interpretation qua interpretation may belong, like authorial intention, to a level of discourse separate from that of the poem. Any interpretation must presumably be tested against the poem itself; it is therefore worth asking if, in Wimsatt's view, interpretive texts would ever have anything other than the "advisory" function he grants to expressions of authorial intention. To treat any expression of interpretation—any "secondary" text—as identical to poetic meaning is, by logical extension of the notion of the "intentional fallacy," to commit an error that we might call the "interpretive fallacy."

The next argument under consideration (4f)—and the one that Wimsatt sees as the most dangerous—arises when "the author's life and canon or some parts of them are urged as a surrounding and controlling context for the poem or some details of it" (p. 215). This argument may be even more critical than Wimsatt is aware, since it raises the question of the relation of context in general (not just the author's life and canon, but language conventions and the reader's horizon of expectations). The only context Wimsatt is ready to accept as controlling the meaning of the poem is, as we saw in 4e, the poem itself. Thus, the implicit logical need for a distinctive kind of meaning, namely the literary, crops up again in connection with Wimsatt's notion of context.

Wimsatt focuses his attack on an example used by Hirsch, the leading proponent of the view being attacked. Hirsch had argued that Blake's "London," especially the last line of the last stanza,

> But most, thr'o midnight streets I hear
> How the youthful Harlot's curse
> Blasts the new-born Infant's tear,
> And blights with plagues the Marriage hearse.
> [*Songs of Innocence and Experience*],

is best understood as a revolutionary statement made by what we know to be a revolutionary writer: "If there were no marriage, there would be no ungratified desires, and therefore no harlots."[7] For Wimsatt "these ideas are silly," putting us "in danger of reading the poem as a pretty bad poem" (p. 217).[8] Wimsatt invokes what remains, I think, the most widely accepted interpretation: venereal disease, contracted from a harlot, invades the marriage bed and is passed on to the children begotten there. The key point is that Wimsatt argues for this reading despite an earlier sketchbook entry by Blake: "Remove away that marriage hearse. . . . You'll quite remove the ancient curse." In short, the very fact that these lines remained in the sketchbook ("where they deserved to remain") is taken to prove that they are not a valid guide to the poem's interpretation. This argument, however, is surely just as intentionalist as Hirsch's, especially as Wimsatt refers us to other equally external sources: "consult the career of an eighteenth-century Londoner like James Boswell or Charles Hanbury Williams" (p. 219).

It is not necessary to take sides in this dispute to observe that taking sides is what it boils down to: one finds either Hirsch's or Wimsatt's interpretation more persuasive, but one is not therefore obliged to accept the critical method it endorses. However, Wimsatt's conclusion seems sound: "a critic [i.e., Hirsch] ought to show that his meaning actually operates in the poem or is generated by it."

But isn't a "balked idea" of the author's the same sort of intentional evidence as one proven to be endorsed by him? And isn't there another problem in the introduction of an ontological chasm between two texts (on personal, evaluative grounds) when, quite often, sketchbooks and the like constitute one of our major sources of poems; that is, why treat one text as a "poem" and another as "not a poem" (and therefore a mere expression of irrelevant intention) if not for the intentionalist reason that one of them was published with the author's blessing or the purely evaluative reason that one is preferable?

These questions are meant to disclose assumptions and show the limits of Wimsatt's argument. But there are even more basic and important questions that arise in connection with the previous discussion. They center around the difficult problem of where the line is to be drawn between what is—or what is in—the text and what is not.

In challenging "the author's life and canon . . . as a surrounding and controlling context for the poem" (p. 219), especially after urging the "context" of the poem for just this purpose, Wimsatt raises the question of just what constitutes the interpretive context of the poem. Quoting his and Beardsley's original essay of 1946, he reaffirms an earlier concession:

> The meaning of words is the history of words and the biography of an author, his use of a word, and the associations which the word has for *him,* are part of the word's history and meaning.

Such a definition of meaning, which could, it seems, be supplemented only by the private associations of individual readers, yields quite a bit indeed. Clearly the sort of meaning described here is contingent upon the reader's competence. Applied as it is now to interpretation rather than evaluation, such a definition makes the very concept of the "intentional fallacy" problematic. "Where," asks Wimsatt in a later essay, quoting the words of a critic of that concept (J. Hillis Miller), "does the context of a poem stop?"[9] What may establish competency in the reader? Expressions of authorial intention? Knowledge of the author's life? If not, why not?

This brings us back to the problem of what I earlier called the "interpretive fallacy." Poetry, not only for Wimsatt but for most of his followers, is distinct from more "practical" forms of discourse, at least in that what is *said* is not what is *meant* literally; that is, meaning is facilitated by "metaphor—the structure most characteristic of concentrated poetry" (*The Verbal Icon,* p. 79). That is why expressions like "marriage hearse" (unlike "funeral hearse" or "marriage bed") seem to stand in need of special interpretation in the first place and why the criteria and results of interpretation can generate so much dispute. Wimsatt's doctrine of the "text itself" is complicated, to say the least, by his theory of interpretation, which posits poetic meaning as figurative, that is, as something other than the face value of the text itself. Either the poetic object is the text itself and poetic meaning (which might then include intention) external to the text or the poetic object is the figurative

meaning, in which case the notion of the concrete text "itself" falls away
(and with it the ability to maintain a stand against either the "intentional"
or the "interpretive" fallacy).

The dilemma just described arises, perhaps, only whenever interpretations are held to be identical to the meanings of poems. Yet Wimsatt
surely would be the last to say that the meaning of "marriage hearse"
was *identical* to the words "marriage bed blighted by venereal disease"
or the like. Hasn't the argument been consistently against the possibility
of the interchangeability of textual equivalents for a single poetic meaning?[10] It would seem that no explication or interpretation (whether the
author's or the critic's) could escape the double bind that applies to
speculation about authorial intention: either the interpretation is not
parallel to the poem itself (in which case the former is inadequate) or it
is (in which case it is superfluous or, at best, merely "advisory").

One thing is clear on the difficult subject of metaphorical (or figurative, or nonliteral) meaning: more is involved than the two terms of
vehicle and tenor. Only the most naive of readers (that is, one unini-
tiated into the convention of reading literature) would mistake the
literal meaning of the vehicle for the meaning of the metaphor. Yet
neither can we identify the meaning of the metaphor with the literal
meaning of the tenor (as might be implied in an explication of the
metaphor) because that would make the explication superior as a piece
of communication to the poem and because we would no longer be
speaking of a metaphor but rather of a literal (albeit different) meaning.
Obviously the relationship of vehicle and tenor provides something that
neither term alone can.[11] Once again, it seems clear that the notion of
the intentional fallacy and the concomitant doctrine of textual autonomy depend on the distinction between literary and nonliterary modes
of meaning. Since the explication of a metaphor (or, by implication, any
symbolic meaning) is not essentially different from the construal of
authorial intention—both, after all, lead to the production of secondary, explicative texts—the notion of the intentional fallacy can be
subsumed under that of the interpretive fallacy.

Wimsatt and Beardsley describe "practical messages" as "successful if
and only if we correctly infer the intention" (*The Verbal Icon*, p. 5). It
seems generally to have been overlooked by their critics that there is a
sense in which this description can be taken as a definition. That is, in a
practical situation, it is the intention—and not the utterance—that
counts. If someone says to me, "You came home late last night," and I
reply, "What is that supposed to mean?," I will probably accept the

speaker's expressed intention—to express concern, to scold, and so forth—as determining the operative meaning of the utterance because it is the intention itself that concerns me. The carry-over of this communicative principle into literary criticism seems to be what prompted Wimsatt and Beardsley to write "The Intentional Fallacy" in the first place. For them, the fact that in ordinary discourse the speaker's intention is of primary importance in no way affects the validity of the notion of the intentional fallacy, because Wimsatt and Beardsley insist that literature means differently and that difference, I will suggest, has to do with the irrelevance of intention itself.

An Overview of the Debate about Intention

Almost without exception, the arguments surrounding the notion of the "intentional fallacy" are based on assumptions about the nature of literary discourse. Literary meaning is seen as either distinct from or of a kind with ordinary communication. If literary meaning is a distinctive mode, then no amount of ordinary communication on the part of the author (however accurate) is relevant. However, such communication may or may not have an influence upon a distinctly literary mode of cognition of meaning. If literary meaning is continuous with ordinary communication, then the question does not arise, since, as in ordinary communication, getting back to the author's intention is the cognitive goal. Put another way, which is often parallel if not identical, what counts in ordinary communication is the meaning "behind" the text; for some, this is also true of literature; for others, literature differs from nonliterature in that what counts in the former is the meaning of the text itself. The problem is complicated by the fact that, for most critics, literature is distinct precisely in that the overt, surface, or nonfigurative meaning of the text is not the one in question. We are left with the unsettling, but not irresolvable, paradox that in literature the text "itself" and the "surface" meaning of the words on the page are not the same.

The following descriptions of attempts to deal with these problems cover most of the major positions (in simplified form) taken with regard to the question of "intention" in American literary studies since approximately 1968, the date of Wimsatt's reconsideration.

GROUP ONE: Intention as plan in the mind of the author.

I.   The meaning of a literary work is identical with the artist's intention, which it is at least one goal of literary criticism to recover (the position Wimsatt and Beardsley explicitly attack).

II.   The meaning of a literary work is qualitatively distinct from the author's plan for or understanding of the work, which—insofar as they are accessible—may duplicate the same information in a nonliterary mode, but are precisely for that reason irrelevant (the position Wimsatt and Beardsley set forth).

IIIa. Nonliterary expressions of intention, though in a mode different from literary meaning, may to a greater or lesser extent influence the experience of that meaning (cf. Wimsatt's argument 4b of 1968).

IIIb. Nonliterary expressions of intention, though in a mode different from literary meaning, play a determinant role in the experience of that meaning (cf. Wimsatt's earlier 4e and 4f).

GROUP TWO: Intention as identical to meaning. The cognition of meaning necessarily involves the construal of intention or, conversely, the author's intention is identical to his or her meaning; intention is therefore embodied in the text itself.

IVa.   Intention is embodied in the text but is nonetheless the author's (who may resolve ambiguity or decide between multiple interpretations). Here it is assumed that there is no categorical distinction between literary and ordinary discourse.

IVb.   Intention is embodied in the text and is independent of the author because of the distinctive nature of literary meaning. (In a variation of IVb, intention is independent of the author but is dependent upon the reader and his or her interpretive constraints.)

Arguments such as roman numeral I are practically nonexistent in the recent literature; that is, the notion of the "intentional fallacy" has gained general credence at least to the extent that opponents of the theory feel compelled to redefine the concept of intention or to challenge Wimsatt and Beardsley's concept of literary meaning on theoretical or historical grounds.[12] Most responses could thus be included in types III and IV. Both accept the notion of "operative" meaning, but both preserve the usefulness of some concept of "intention," the first by arguing that intention, itself extrinsic, has an intrinsic effect; the second, that intention is itself intrinsic to that meaning. Both of these positions are anticipated and, to a certain extent, defused by Wimsatt and Beardsley. (E. D. Hirsch and Stanley Fish, whose arguments fall under IVa and IVb, respectively, are discussed in subsequent chapters and so omitted below.)

The best place to begin a discussion of the controversy is perhaps with the argument made by Suresh Raval that there is no controversy or, at least, that the controversy is irresolvable. He argues that the dispute between the genetic method and a belief in its fallaciousness is, to borrow a term from W. B. Gallie, "essentially contested"; that is, neither point of view can "be logically refuted or reduced to some other concept."[13] The reason for this is that each side in the controversy is arguing from a theory of literary art that is not itself subject to logical refutation or verification: Wimsatt and Beardsley's 1946 essay is, for Raval, "part of a larger, modernist attack on romanticism and its critical principles" (literature as primarily expressive), an attempt to view literature in the neoclassical vein as primarily mimetic (p. 263).

Raval goes on to argue that "a construal of intention is implied in an act of interpretation." But, he says, this does not mean that he is settling the issue by calling both sides intentionalist. Rather, the "dispute centers on what constitutes the correct mode of such a construal" (p. 274). Even though Raval believes that "there is no single correct mode of construing intention" (just as theories of art are not exhausted by the romantic and neoclassical viewpoints), he assumes nonetheless that a *literary* meaning is construed. If this "construed" intention is consistent with that "realized" in the poem as described by Wimsatt and Beardsley in 1946—and I find nothing in Raval's essay to indicate that it is not—then his arguments do not contradict the theory of a distinctly poetic meaning upon which, as I have argued, the doctrine of the intentional fallacy depends. The Wimsatt of 1946 would certainly object to the implied logical priority of external intention to realized intention, but by 1968 the "advisory" function of such intention had been, though somewhat grudgingly, granted.

We find an interesting variation on this "advisory" intentionalism (IIIa) in an essay by Ingo Seidler.[14] Seidler seems to accept the New Critical demand that the meaning of the poem be found in the poem. However, in addition to stressing that the advisory function of authorial intention may be essential (as in Goethe's use of the word *Natur* or Rilke's use of *Verwandlung*), Seidler raises the very interesting question of whether the poetic mode of meaning need necessarily be limited to the single work in isolation.

Logicians make a distinction between intentional objects of narrower or wider conceptual compass and, inversely, of more or less specific contents. . . . But to consider objects of narrower compass and more specific contents "more real" than their more inclusive counterparts is philosophically objectionable as well as methodologically self-defeating.

In other words, Seidler leaves open the possibility of there being "poems" (in Wimsatt and Beardsley's sense) or poetic objects that go beyond individual texts to include semantic implications to be derived from an entire oeuvre, an entire *Zeitgeist*. [15]

One might object that we recognize texts as separate entities in the first place because of their high degree of unity and self-containment, that that is a part of what is meant by "poem." Wimsatt would surely argue that a poem which required knowledge of the author's idiosyncratic use of a word was to that extent an ineffectively realized poem. But there seem to be few theoretical (as opposed to practical) objections to admitting the argument that poetic unity and self-containment might be realized at a higher level as a legitimate expansion of Wimsatt and Beardsley's theory of literary meaning.

Wimsatt would probably object very strongly to a logical extension of the "advisory" function of avowed or biographical intention; namely, that there are situations in which such intentions actually determine the realized meaning of the poem (IIIb). Yet I do not think this view is really incompatible with his theory of poetic meaning as long as it is remembered that such intentions are qualitatively distinct from the meaning realized. In other words, determinant intentions are not simply offered as evidence for meaning; they actually produce or at least structure meaning.

There would seem to be at least three distinct types of intentionally determinate meaning: nonliterary, poorly integrated literary, and literary. Launching an attack on the doctrine of the intentional fallacy, Peter D. Juhl provides us with an example of the first type. [16] "But surely sometimes an expressed or inferred intention will be an important influence on what we take a sentence to mean, even if we would say that those words could not 'normally' be used to mean so and so." Juhl relates an anecdote told by Arnold Isenberg. [17]

A Japanese colleague with whom I once shared an office would sometimes enter when I was there and say, "Please, don't make trouble." I could easily interpret this: "Please do not trouble yourself on my account."

It could be argued that Mr. Isenberg, by dint of convention, simply understood his colleague to *say* what he says he understood him to *mean*.

But even if we grant that intention determines meaning in this instance, it is not clear why Wimsatt and Beardsley's position is threatened. In 1946 they granted that, in the case of nonliterary discourse, interpretation depends on correctly inferring the author's intention; that is in fact precisely what distinguishes it from literary discourse (the distinctive nature of which Juhl dismisses out of hand, p. 11). Of the "at least two important distinguishing characteristics of imaginative literature," Juhl finds the second ("the prominence of suggestion and connotation") "to have little bearing on the question at hand," despite the parallel he himself points out between this quality and Beardsley's 1958 definition of literature as evincing a "prominence of suggestion and connotation,"[18] and despite Wimsatt's attempt to tie their semantic theory closely to metaphor. However, literature seems in some way not to mean what it says (whether it is a question of metaphor or fiction). Instead of addressing this problem, Juhl defends his determinant-intentionalist viewpoint only against Wimsatt and Beardsley's "distinction between speaker and author" (p. 11).

Juhl's argument is as follows: the speaker is distinct and in some sense independent of the author, but when the latter expresses his intentions, he is not usurping the place of the speaker, but rather clarifying what he "intended the speaker to mean" (p. 12):

> the distinction between speaker and author has no influence on
> the relevance of an explicit statement of intention, since the latter
> is by definition evidence about the speaker.

In other words, the words of the poem are meant by the speaker and the speaker is meant by the author; hence, the distinction between speaker and author does not, for Juhl, invalidate the evidence of authorial intention because it must be understood to be evidence *about* the speaker.

Juhl is right to point out that the author's voice in the poem goes beyond that of the speaker, who is himself "spoken." But he misunderstands Wimsatt and Beardsley if he thinks their distinction is limited to the speaker or narrator alone:

> We ought to impute the thoughts and attitudes of the poem
> immediately to the dramatic speaker, and if to the author at all,
> only by an act of biographical inference [*The Verbal Icon*, p. 5].

Wimsatt and Beardsley do, it is true, seem reluctant about this last point, but Wayne Booth has developed it nicely (and in a way not at all inconsistent with the arguments of "The Intentional Fallacy," which admit of realized intentions) in his concept of the "implied author." Booth speaks of the literary work of art

> as the product of a choosing, evaluating person rather than . . . a self-existing thing. The "implied author" chooses, consciously or unconsciously, what we read; we infer him as an ideal, literary, created version of the real man; he is the sum of his own choices.[19]

The concept of the "implied author" has close affinities with the notion that meaning necessarily involves the construal of intention. But such a concept argues for, rather than against, the logical and semantic priority of the literary text by identifying implication as one element of the text's realized meaning. Wimsatt in fact anticipates not only Booth but Wolfgang Iser, who further develops Booth's theory in the notion of the "implied reader."[20] Wimsatt thus provides textually operative (and so "literary") alternatives to both the "intentional" and the "affective" fallacies.

> The actual reader of a poem is something like a reader over another reader's shoulder; he reads through the dramatic reader, the person to whom the full tone of the poem is addressed in the fictional situation [*The Verbal Icon*, p. xv].

> Both reader and dramatic audience are assimilated into the implicit structure of the poem's meaning. At the fully cognitive level of appreciation we unite in our own minds both speaker and audience [p. xvi].

The "implied author" is then distinct from both the "speaker" (in the narrow sense understood by Juhl) or narrator (cf. Booth, p. 73) *and* the historical author. Juhl makes the first distinction, but overlooks the second, thus begging the question at a higher level. The "author" is necessary to the construal of the text's meaning, but he is not qualitatively the same as the historical author of an "explicit statement of intention" (except in the sense that that one, too, is "implied"). That Juhl has in mind the former, "implied," author is clear from another of his arguments.

> When we discard some explicit statement of intention, we are, I think, inferring the speaker's intention on the basis of evidence which we regard in that instance as more reliable, namely, the linguistic (and/or non-linguistic) context rather than the explicit statement of intention [p. 10].

Moreover, the fact that, when we dismiss such a statement,

> we would say that the author was mistaken as to his intention shows
> quite clearly that we take, in that case, the text as better evidence of
> his intention, rather than that his intention is irrelevant [p. 17].

Clearly an operative intention is in question here and, hence, an operative or implied author. Wimsatt and Beardsley's first axiom of 1946 has already taken Juhl's argument into account: "the man we were in search of was not the man we wanted" (*The Verbal Icon*, p. 6).

In any case, Juhl seems to accept Wimsatt and Beardsley's basic semantic distinction by arguing consistently that intention is a part of poetic meaning; if he insists, as does E. D. Hirsch, on saying that this intention is the author's, it is nonetheless not the sort of intention that Wimsatt and Beardsley attack, since they are careful to distinguish that kind from external intention.

The second sort of determinant intention—the poorly integrated— could be seen, for example, in any sort of symbolic meaning that is arbitrary rather than necessary. Such would be the case whenever we are told (by the poet or someone else) that a particularly obscure passage represents "death" or the like and our best effort fails to let us "see" it. Other examples would include the sort of everyday arbitrary symbolization that we see in the fact that a red light means "stop" or that the thirteen stripes in the American flag represent the thirteen colonies. (Note I do not say that symbols could ever be other than arbitrary; I merely wish to point out that, in proposing the notion of the intentional fallacy, Wimsatt and Beardsley assume that they could be.)

This second sort of determinant intentionalism seems answered by Wimsatt and Beardsley's discussion in 1946 of the allusions in (clarified by the "Notes" to) *The Wasteland*. Insofar as the notes facilitate the poem's understanding, they may be regarded as "part of the poem," but parts which are loosely integrated and hence argue a weakness or lack of unity in the poem (*The Verbal Icon*, p. 16). Once the semantic distinction between literary and ordinary meaning that allows Wimsatt and Beardsley to speak of the poem "itself" is granted, their reasoning here appears to be the last word and could be used to refute other arguments for the "advisory" function of intention. Insofar as the poem cannot be interpreted without external evidence, it is a weak poem.

Given the above line of reasoning, we might expect that the third kind of determinant intention—which might be termed the literary (because the effect in question is produced by the work itself)—would be, from

the Wimsatt/Beardsley point of view, a contradiction in terms. One
version of this argument (attributed, interestingly enough, to Beardsley) is set forth by Joel J. Kupperman.[21]

> It is often said that in appreciating something aesthetically we as it
> were put a frame around it. Presumably this is the point of putting
> Campbell soup cans and *objets trouvés* in museums, or labelling as
> art things that normally would not be considered art. The artists
> who do this are attempting to get us to see aesthetically what we
> would not normally see aesthetically: the very act of putting
> something in a museum, or labelling it as art, can accomplish this.
> The vision that putting a frame around something helps us to
> achieve is of the object as having an interesting character of its
> own, set off from its surroundings.

One could argue against this view that "pop" art and "found" art are
exceptions to the rule of the "intentional fallacy," since they belong to
historical movements in which art is defined in a certain way, one which
deliberately violates the expectation that art-objects will be distinct
from ordinary ones, an expectation which is itself part of another
historical notion of art. One is free, that is, to object that the standards
of Dada (if that is not a contradiction in terms) do not touch those of
New Criticism, or even that works in the Dadaist tradition are inherently "poorly integrated" because of their merely intentional determination. On the other hand, if "framing" truly converts latrines and soup
cans into works of art, then they are no longer ordinary objects. That is,
although an intention—taken up by the reader—is the ultimate cause
of an aesthetic affect, Wimsatt and Beardsley's demand that intention
be operative is met.

As a universal aesthetic principle, the intentional-frame theory, like
Wimsatt and Beardsley's semantic theory, amounts to a conception of
the nature of art and so enjoys the dubious privilege of being "essentially
contested." An extreme example of such a view is developed by Ina
Loewenberg, who goes so far as to reverse completely Wimsatt and
Beardsley's notion that aesthetic meaning is independent of authorial
intention. Loewenberg argues that works of literary art are distinct
from ordinary discourse precisely because intentions are central for
identifying the former and, for the most part, irrelevant for identifying
the latter.[22] Put simply, Loewenberg's argument is as follows. Utterances are ordinarily meaningful because they conform to convention;

that is, they may be construed without further knowledge of the speaker's intentions. Art works, on the other hand, depend on such knowledge. A beautiful mountain is not a work of art; however, an object we know to be intended to be viewed as such a work, however "bizarre" or undeserving of "aesthetic approval," we accept as a work of art.

Literary texts, as Loewenberg goes on to argue, belong to a group of

> utterances . . . which . . . cannot be correctly understood unless understood as intended by the speaker. These utterances are instances of irony, overstatement and understatement, punning and other humorous devices, and metaphor. In making an utterance of one of these kinds the speaker intends to say the exact words he does say but he intends them to mean something other than their usual meanings [p. 44].

However, the writer is, suggest Loewenberg, limited even here by the need for a certain amount of semantic autonomy—"the face-value meanings of the words" (p. 45)—at the literal level.

Furthermore, there is an important difference between an external intention which identifies and one which *interprets* or *judges* something already identified as a work of art. We might admit that the reader's aesthetic-response mechanism must be triggered by some sort of external cue without having to admit explicit intentions as evidence for saying anything further about the particular work in question. In fact, what triggers an aesthetic response may have nothing to do with that response. If the "intentional fallacy" can logically be extended to the "interpretive fallacy," it might well cover the knowledge *that* one is reading a poem (the first step in any interpretation), as opposed to the knowledge that comes *from* reading a poem. I might not call a mountain a work of art and yet give that name to an uninteresting lump of clay, but, assuming my aesthetic-response potentiality is somehow cued, there is no reason to assume that a view of a mountain is a radically different experience from seeing another physical object such as a block of wood that I have been told to consider aesthetically.

Finally, if the intention at work in the identification of art works is to be identified with a certain kind of (aesthetic) response, then the intention is clearly of the "operative" or "construed" variety. That returns us to the question of integration as a criterion of success in art: Wimsatt and Beardsley's point would seem to be that such necessary components of poetic meaning as being-recognizable-as-a-poem must be in the text itself.

The Author as Interpreter

The great majority of intentionalist arguments since the firm establishment of American New Criticism have been predicated on the notion
that "intentions" can or must be embodied within texts themselves.[23]
Wimsatt, as we have seen, makes it clear in 1968 that the article of 1946
rejected a certain kind of intention (defined as external) and accepted
intentions "found in, or inferred from, the work itself" (p. 210). Never-
theless, there are some variations on this theme that do not seem
directly anticipated by Wimsatt and Beardsley and that it is therefore
useful to consider (saving the arguments of Hirsch and Fish for a more
detailed consideration in chapters two and three).

Michael Hancher has attempted to describe a sort of internal intention which is nonetheless the author's. In "Three Kinds of Intention,"
Hancher distinguishes "programmatic" intentions (the author's plan to
do something), "active" intentions (this corresponds closely to the understanding of meaning as the construal of intention), and "final"
intentions (the author's plan to cause some sort of effect).[24]

By subdividing the first term of Wimsatt and Beardsley's distinction
between intention and text, Hancher hopes to recuperate for literary
studies part of what he thinks they want to exclude. This part is the
author's "active" intention:

> Active intentions characterize the actions that the author, at the
> time he finishes his text, understands himself to be performing in
> that text. . . . Such intentions . . . bear on the text and shape
> its "meaning" at the moment of completion. The author for his
> part need and indeed can do nothing further to realize an active
> intention; it is realized in the act of intention itself.

Wimsatt and Beardsley, according to Hancher, exclude all intention as
plan in favor of the text itself; he argues, however, that "active" intentions
are a part of the author's meaning that is operative within the text itself.
The problem with the concept of "active" intention as an interpretive
principle is, if I understand it correctly, that it corresponds to the concept
of "operative" intention only for one interpreter: the author himself.

Hancher seems to overlook Wimsatt and Beardsley's acceptance of
inferred intentions. In a sense, they have already made and granted the
distinction he makes; they simply deny that operative intentions are
authorial in a way that goes beyond the text itself or, if they correspond
to expressed intentions, that the latter are necessary. At the same time,

Hancher overlooks the fact that Wimsatt and Beardsley do indeed exclude what Hancher terms "active" intentions (in another sense); that is, for them the author's judgment of his own work is as inadmissable "at the time he finishes his text" (surely a hazy, inadequately conceptualized "time") as at any other time. Wimsatt (1968, p. 213) relates an amusing anecdote in which Samuel Johnson "corrects" Goldsmith's explanation of what he (Goldsmith) had meant by the use of a certain word in "The Traveller." It is possible to take Hancher's "active" intention in both these senses because he himself seems to be unclear on the point; in fact, the notion of "active" intention begs the very question it is meant to allay: does such information belong to the author or to the text?

The only way for operative intentions to be unequivocally authorial would be if the author, at a certain cognitive (rather than temporal) moment—the moment when an idea is realized in the conventional medium of language—becomes a reader of his own text. However, the author is, as René Wellek has observed,[25] only another reader of the text. And however accurate his own experience of the text's meaning might be, when he comes to convey this experience in critical discourse, he becomes only another critic and the gap between his two selves (author and interpreter) widens.[26] If the author's authority is to lie in the fact that he is also an active reader of his own text (which is what Hancher's after-the-fact "active" intention amounts to), it is difficult to see why the explication of any critic should not be (at least potentially) equally authoritative. "No doubt the author is likely to be a good guide," admits Wimsatt (1968, p. 211), but like the pronouncements of any interpreter, his words ultimately stand or fall on how they compare to the poem itself. The author's "active" intentions would be authoritative only if there were nothing problematic about—and hence no need for—interpretation. But then there would be no need for authority because the meaning of the poem would be immediately and unequivocally accessible.

Something like an extreme view of the author as reader emerges from an essay by Jeremy Lane. Lane, citing Maurice Blanchot, suggests that, at least in some cases, it is the author who is written by his text. (This view also has certain similarities to the view that all intentions are implied, that is, construed from texts.)

> Stephen [Dedalus], as subject and perceiving, feeling consciousness, importantly creates his world, the world of the fiction, and thus authorises his author, James Joyce.[27]

The writer is primarily a reader, argues Lane: even for the author the meaning of the text must be, in a profound sense, internal:

> this kind of fiction claims a fundamental autonomy. The fiction is, in a double sense, the writer's search for self, Proust's *moi profond*, a search which must, however, be conducted by means of an alterity, at base that necessitated by language itself.

Lane argues, in effect, that the writer is in the same epistemological situation as any other reader. Lane is, to be sure, concerned here with "modern literature in particular" (that is, his theory is a historical, an "essentially contested" theory of literature). His position differs from that of Hancher in the implied logical priority of "active" intentions over "programmatic" ones: what one succeeds in meaning determines our concept of who is doing the meaning. Lane's argument, if valid, changes the picture with regard to the question of "authority" radically. On the one hand, it is indeed the author's active intention that gives the text its meaning, at least for the author himself. On the other, the text is truly autonomous in the sense that the author of it is himself, even for himself, implied.

These seemingly contradictory points are perhaps resolved by another implication of Lane's argument: that of a realignment of our view of the relationship of text, author, and reader. In a practical, or even temporal, sense, the meaning of a work goes from author to text to reader. But logically the meaning of a work could be described in terms of at least two cognitive relationships: that of the active perception of poetic meaning (which we might call the act of a "reader," though it might be performed by the author) and that of relating poetic meaning in any one of a number of ways to extrinsic information expressed in nonliterary discourse (which might include anything from expressions of authorial intention to the reader's interpretation). In other words, both living, historical author and living, historical reader stand in the same relationship to literary texts: either can function as reader *or* as interpreter; both struggle on more or less equal terms within the medium of language to find the meaning of the poem, that is, to find the poem itself. The act of creation might itself be a kind of reading.

These two functions (and the conflict they engender) are discussed by Stein Haugom Olsen, who points out the logical dilemma which arises from the admission of "external evidence for the intentions expressed by literary works."

If we allow authorial statements of intention as a supplement to literary works, we have to deal with two expressions. The first is the literary work of art. The second is an utterance which clarifies the first expression. This latter utterance must be superior to the first at least in the respect of clarifying the intention behind the first utterance. That is, the second expression must express the intention better than the part of the first expression for which it counts as a clarification. If the second expression is not superior in this way, it does not have a job to do and will be discarded. . . . We shall ultimately have to take the speaker's word for what he meant if his behavior is not inconsistent with what he says. If he says that his second and explanatory utterance better represent his intention than the literary work he used as the first expression of his intention, we shall have to accept that. But this effectively removes any justification for the use of a concept of literature.[28]

Olsen's willingness to let the author be the final authority does not blind him to the problem involved with such a view, namely that if we accept the author's act of interpretation, we seem to reject the poem itself. We should note, however, that his point applies just the same to the secondary texts produced by critics: they too call the locus and status of literary meaning into question.

Summary

Because ordinary meaning is by nature identical to authorial intention, the notion of the intentional fallacy—in excluding assertions about that intention—presupposes that literature means in a way that is not ordinary, not determined by the author's intention but rather by properties of the text itself. The question immediately arises as to why the author's intention, which is surely meaningful, should necessarily be distinct from the meaning of the text. The answer is that the notion of authorial intention, as Wimsatt and Beardsley understand it, is limited to cases in which the author's meaning is explicitly distinct from textual meaning because the former is expressed in a secondary text (whether authorial statements or intentionalist speculation) claiming semantic equivalence with the latter. Authorial intention is thus a special case of the ascription of meaning to a text, that is, the substitution of one text for another in an assertion of semantic equivalence. That this tendency is pervasive enough to merit the label "ordinary meaning" is evidenced by the fact that the process in question goes under the name "interpretation." Indeed, one has difficulty imagining an alternative. Wimsatt and Beardsley's implicit claim is that, in literature, meaning (rather than a nexus of semantically equivalent expressions) is of primary importance. The notion of the intentional fallacy is thus subsumable under the broader categorization of what I have called the interpretive fallacy. However, we are left with at least three unanswered questions. What is the nature of literary (that is, simple) meaning? How is it that literary texts operate at that level? How can literature peculiarly operate at the level of simple meaning when it appears to be a peculiar feature of literary texts that their simple, surface meaning is not the one that is operative?

Obviously, any theory of literature which does not recognize it as having a distinct mode of meaning will have no trouble making a case for the intentionalist viewpoint. However, Wimsatt and Beardsley's exclusion of the author in favor of the text itself must be recognized as a heuristic exaggeration (or metaphor). The literary text is, as Wimsatt himself points out (*The Verbal Icon*, p. xvii), not an object but an act of communication. Wimsatt and Beardsley never argue that literary texts do not mean what their authors planned, desired, and understood them to mean (though they are perhaps pressured into defending that possibility); rather, they insist that this meaning is not to be judged on the basis of other (nonliterary) expressions. We should thus distinguish not so much between intention and meaning as between two sorts of intention, one imputed (therefore meaningful in an ordinary way) and one "realized" (therefore meaningful in a literary way). As I will argue in chapter four, such a distinction may help not only to illuminate the sense in which it is eminently useful to consider the literary mode of meaning as distinct from the nonliterary; it can also connect the notion of the intentional (or interpretive) fallacy with the question of referentiality in different types of discourse.

2

Validity in Authority:
E. D. Hirsch

The Necessity of Authority

Hirsch begins his "defense of the author" by challenging the distinction between what an author means and what his or her text means. The argument that "the meaning of a text changes—even for the author"[1] Hirsch meets with the assertion that what changes for the author is not the meaning, but the meaning of the meaning.[2] The doctrine of "semantic autonomy" set forth by Wimsatt and Beardsley is, insists Hirsch, properly applicable only to evaluation, not interpretation: what is left when the author's meaning is disregarded is not the "text itself" but simply some *reader's* meaning (pp. 10–14). (Arguing thus, Hirsch rejects the idea of the neutral ground sought by Wimsatt and Beardsley in the hypostatization of the poetic object and implies that they fall victim to what they themselves describe as the "affective fallacy.") The view that "the author's meaning is inaccessible" Hirsch counters by pointing out that it is in the nature of meaning (as opposed to private experiences of meaning) to *be* accessible through the public medium of language (pp. 14–19). The assertion that "the author often does not know what he means" is not to the point, says Hirsch, because meaning something and knowing that one means it are different: it is possible to intend something without being explicitly conscious of it or without being able to explain it (pp. 19–23).

Hirsch's insistence that what we know of the author's meaning is both irrelevant and author-itative (that is, that the author is not simply another interpreter) is based on his very important distinction between "meaning" and "significance," which he explains as follows:

> *Meaning* is that which is represented by a text: it is what the author
> meant by his use of a particular sign sequence; it is what the signs
> represent. *Significance,* on the other hand, names a relationship
> between that meaning and a person, or conception, or indeed
> anything imaginable [p. 8].

When the author's intention does not seem to correspond to the text, it
is the "significance" that is at variance, not the "meaning," which remains stable. Interestingly, in the very process of challenging the notion
of what he calls "semantic autonomy" (Wimsatt and Beardsley's hypostatized poetic object), Hirsch argues for a kind of textual stability that is
beyond the author's ability to change simply at will: "Clearly what
changes for them [authors] is not the meaning of the work, but rather
their relationship to that meaning" (p. 8). In fact, says Hirsch, if it were
not for the stability of textual meaning, which serves as a substratum, we
would have no way of discussing the plurality of textual significances in
the first place.

Since "the text has to represent *somebody's* meaning—if not the author's, then the critic's" (p. 3), Hirsch takes it for granted that the only
rational choice for the interpreter is to opt for the author's meaning.
The text has to represent somebody's meaning, because "meaning is an
affair of consciousness not of words" (p. 4), and if the critic's meaning
were permitted to prevail over the author's (as for example in the
doctrine of the "best" reading), then "the critic would be the author of
the best meaning" (p. 5). "Whenever meaning is attached to a sequence
of words," continues Hirsch, "it is impossible to escape an author."

This conclusion leaves open the possibility that there would be as
many legitimate authors as there are interpreters, of course, but this is
the very notion that Hirsch wants to challenge. Indeed, it is this very
possibility that prompts Hirsch to plead for authority.

> Almost any word can, under the conventions of language, legiti-
> mately represent more than one complex of meaning. A word
> sequence means nothing in particular until somebody either
> means something by it or understands something from it [p. 4].

Because this is true, we are faced with a dilemma in which the author's
meaning is the only way out:

> For if the meaning of a text is not the author's, then no interpretation
> can possibly correspond to the meaning of the text, since the text can
> have no determinate or determinable meaning [p. 5].

Thus, Hirsch also adheres to a notion of the "objectivity" of textual meaning, but it is quite different from that of Wimsatt and Beardsley. They originally developed the notion of the "intentional fallacy" in order to challenge historico-biographical judgments of poetic *value*.[3] Wimsatt later extended the concept retroactively to cover *interpretation*. Hirsch is willing to admit the validity of Wimsatt and Beardsley's theory concerning questions of evaluation, because for him evaluation is strictly a matter of "significance." It is, for him, external to the poem in the way "intention" is external for them. "However," he goes on to say, "the intentional fallacy has no proper application whatever to verbal meaning" (p. 12). Evaluation, which is variable, itself presupposes a prior level of stable meaning. Whereas Wimsatt and Beardsley tend to equate the achievement of poetic meaning itself with value, putting a premium on successful integration within the poetic mode, Hirsch keeps meaning and poetic value distinct.

In arguing this way, Hirsch seems to sacrifice another sacred cow (like determinacy above) for the purpose of saving the temple itself. Not only do poems, taken in themselves, have no determinate meaning, but whatever makes a poem good or bad seems to be something outside the poem itself.[4] Both of these sacrifices—gambits might be a better word—are related to Hirsch's rejection of the notion that literature is in any profound way distinct from other modes of discourse. That notion, as I have argued, underlies the concept of the intentional fallacy; indeed, the concept of the intentional fallacy and its accompanying category of the "internal" or "intrinsic" would be meaningless *without* the notion of a distinct literary mode. It is interesting, then, that Hirsch's distinction between "meaning" and "significance" is useful to him precisely because it gives him a working concept of internality, that is, of the text itself. And, as do Wimsatt and Beardsley, Hirsch develops his theory of literary meaning on the basis of a principle of exclusion: what is "external" or "extrinsic" to the poem itself (for example, changes in its significance for the author) cannot be cited as evidence that the poem is not the stable representation of an intention.

Meaning as Sharable Intention

Hirsch's first line of argument, discussed in the previous section, is designed to lead from the "chaos" of unavoidable indeterminacy to the practical necessity of admitting authority. The second, to which I will turn now, seeks to define meaning as something stable and sharable by equating meaning with authorial intention. This second line of argument is in a sense contradictory to the first, because it attempts to show that meaning *is* determinate.

> Verbal meaning is whatever someone has willed to convey by a particular sequence of linguistic signs and which can be conveyed (shared) by means of those linguistic signs [p. 31].

This quotation shows the two main points of Hirsch's second argument side by side. Having relegated whatever is variable (including literariness) to the realm of significance in order to argue the stability of "meaning," Hirsch now attempts to prove that a determinate meaning is indeed communicable. Hirsch's distinction between "meaning" and "significance" cannot be understood apart from what Hirsch acknowledges as his philosophical heritage. The philosophical backgrounds of his theory are sketched out in several appendices at the end of *Validity in Interpretation*.

Appendix I ("Objective Interpretation")[5] shows Hirsch's debt to Frege and Husserl who, in different ways, support the claim that

> understanding (and therefore interpretation, in the strict sense of the word) is both logically and psychologically prior to what is generally called criticism [p. 209].

Criticism may suffer from a lack of determinacy, argues Hirsch, but interpretation does not because it is rooted in "meaning" (p. 210). "Interpretation" and "criticism" are, for Hirsch, the acts that correspond to the construal, respectively, of "meaning" and "significance." These two activities are different because they have different objects (p. 211). The object of interpretation is textual meaning; the object of criticism is the relation of that interpreted meaning to something— anything—else. Criticism could thus be called, though Hirsch never puts it this way, the interpretation of interpretation.

The distinction between "meaning" and "significance" originates, Hirsch tells us, from an essay by Gottlob Frege entitled "Über Sinn and Bedeutung,"[6] where Frege "demonstrated that although the meaning of two texts may be different, their referent or truth-value may be identical" (p. 211).[7] Hirsch gives the example of the sentence "Scott is the author of *Waverly*," where "Scott" and "author" have the same "reference," but different "meanings." The meaning/significance distinction, says Hirsch further, "is a special case of Husserl's general distinction between the inner and outer horizons of any meaning" (p. 211):

The relation between an act of awareness and its object Husserl calls "intention," using the term in its traditional philosophical sense, which is much broader than that of "purpose" and is roughly equivalent to "awareness" [p. 218].

Hirsch goes on to explain that "verbal meaning is simply a special kind of intentional object." What is important here for Hirsch is "that *different* intentional acts (on different occasions) each 'intend' an *identical* intentional object." Similarly, various expressions, each of which has a different *Sinn*, may all refer to the same object, that is, have the same *Bedeutung*. Hirsch thus concludes:

> Verbal meaning, being an intentional object, is unchanging, that is, it may be reproduced by different intentional acts and remains self-identical through all these reproductions. Verbal meaning is the sharable content of the speaker's intentional object [p. 219].

Hirsch goes on to explain, considering Husserl's perceptual model in more detail:

> Normally, when I perceive a box, I am explicitly conscious of only three sides, and yet I assert with full confidence (although I might be wrong) that I "intend" a box, an object with *six* sides [p. 221].

Someone else might see the box from another angle, might even see three completely different sides, and yet intend the "same" box that I do. In fact, suggests Hirsch, if this were not possible, there would be no way of recognizing different perspectives *as* perspectives-upon-a-box. Furthermore, the three unseen sides belong to the intention no less than what is immediately visible: they are implied in the intention of the three sides as three *sides of a box*. Similarly, says Hirsch, the "unconscious implications" of an author's utterance are "intended," as indeed are all of the implied (and hence figurative or "literary") meanings of that utterance, even though they may not be expressly stated or endorsed.[8]

These two components of the intentional object—the explicit and the implicit (neither of which is equal to the object itself)—constitute the "inner" and "outer" horizons, respectively, of perceptual (or textual) meaning. The "outer horizon," furthermore, corresponds to the context within which (or as a part of which) the "inner horizon" must be understood. Hirsch is thus able at once to maintain the objectivity and stability of textual meaning and to reject the argument that literary texts (unlike other forms of discourse) do not ultimately mean what they literally say. (It will be remembered that Hirsch denies that literary meaning is unique.)

Hirsch also presents a solution to the problem of the relation of meaning to context (a question raised by Wimsatt and Beardsley's postulation of an autonomous "text"); for Hirsch, they are identical (that is, meaning is equivalent to the total intentional object, not just what is given explicitly or, for that matter, implicitly). We are aware not of discrete visible or invisible sides but of a whole box. Thus, it is the words on the page, the "text itself" (like the visible sides of the box) which are incomplete according to Hirsch's view and not, as Wimsatt and Beardsley insist, the author's intention. Expressions or inferences of intention have the same status as the words on the page (just as the invisible sides of the box have the same status, with regard to the whole, as the visible): neither is in itself sufficient; either is a legitimate perspective on the meaning in question. One point on which both camps seem to agree is that meaning must be operative and not merely imputed (whether by an expression or inference of intention or by the hypostatized words on the page).

Hirsch's equation of meaning and context is developed further in his Appendix II, where he makes clear the distinction between his own view and that of Hans Georg Gadamer, who sets forth a comparable theory of context in *Wahrheit und Methode*. [9] According to Hirsch, Gadamer, strongly influenced by the existential turn Heidegger gave to Husserl's theory of intentionality, develops a mistaken notion of the interpretive horizon as *Vorurteil* ("prejudice," p. 258). Gadamer understands the horizon in terms of prejudice because of the apparent paradox that Dilthey described as the "hermeneutic circle," namely, that "we *cannot* understand a part as such until we have a sense of the whole" (p. 259) and vice versa. Hirsch suggests that, by unduly emphasizing half of the circle, Gadamer is led to view the horizon or context as preceding the entire act of interpretation of meaning (rather than just the interpretation of the parts) and, hence, to take a skeptical view of interpretation according to which one could understand only what one already knew or believed, whether as the result of one's historical situation or personal expectations. [10] How, then, does one understand something new, something communicated by another, or alter one's view of a text's meaning?

Hirsch urges an understanding of *Vorurteil* much more in keeping, he feels, with the phenomenological origins of the concept, namely, as "pre-understanding":

. . . this preliminary perception is always vague since it is, by
necessity, without parts, unarticulated. It is an adumbration, a
pre-apprehension rather than an articulated understanding [p. 259].

"Adumbration" is the usual translation of *Abschattung*, a word that
occurs frequently in Husserl's perceptual model and that refers either
to the process by which the intentional object emerges as a unity in a
multiplicity of perspectives or to the imaginary projection of those
perspectives (like the unseen sides of the box) in the intention of a whole
object. Thus, *Vorurteil*, or the interpretive horizon, would be equivalent to—rather than a necessary prerequisite for—the intentional
object as a whole, before it is critically articulated. Hirsch seems to fault
Gadamer for not distinguishing between what Hirsch calls "meaning
and consciousness of meaning" (p. 22). Gadamer sees meaning as
preceded by prejudice (says Hirsch); Hirsch sees it as succeeded by
critical self-awareness. As we will see later, Hirsch understands the
intentional object to be determined as much by its parts as by its
provisional wholeness—he believes that the hermeneutic circle can be
broken.

According to the notion of "pre-understanding," meaning (in a conventional sense) seems to pre-exist or conform to itself (depending on
one's point of view): understanding is either prejudiced or—and Hirsch
seems to incline to a position that might lead to this second view—
superfluous. Indeed, if understanding is the critical self-awareness that
follows the "unarticulated pre-apprehension," then it would seem rather
close to what Hirsch calls "consciousness of meaning" (which he distinguishes from "meaning" and dismisses as a question of "significance").

The paradox of meaning's pre-existence, which is nothing less than
the paradox of the hermeneutic circle itself, leads Hirsch to two concepts that I take to be attempts to account for that pre-existence in a
nonparadoxical way: "type" and "intrinsic genre." In Hirsch's later
theory, expounded in *The Aims of Interpretation* (1976), these two notions, both static, are supplanted by a third, dynamic one: *corrigible
schemata*. The idea underlying these two notions is a complex one,
preserving some of the qualities of both "individual" and "species"
(normally we think only of the latter in connection with "type" or
"genre"). In Appendix II ("An Excursus on Types") Hirsch defines his
subject as follows:

I consider a type to be a mental object or, if one prefers, an idea.
The essential feature of a type idea is its ability to subsume more

than one experience and therefore to represent more than one experience [p. 265].

Already to say that a "type" is a mental object is to extend the concept of the typical to individual experience. Why, then, is the notion of typicality necessary at all? When Hirsch says that "the essential feature of a type idea is its ability to subsume more than one experience," he obviously has in mind Husserl's concept of "intention," as Hirsch understands it. Because mental objects are constituted (adumbrated) rather than given, there must be some principle of organization at work. Because they remain stable throughout changes in time (memory) and space (perspective), this principle must be repeatable; because it is repeatable, it must be possible to abstract from various experiences of the object whatever it is that they have in common. This theoretical possibility is, I think, what leads Hirsch to associate meaning with "types": the operative notion here is not generalizability, but (as a somewhat problematic logical consequence of repeatability) sharability.

Hirsch does not deal with the question of whether each new experience must not also be a new mental object (after all, if a visual image is a mental object, then a cube seen from the top is a different mental object from one that presents three sides). If such is the case, then there would theoretically be as many "types" as possible experiences, weakening somewhat the notion of "type" for Hirsch's purpose of arguing sharability and determinacy. In any case, there appears to be no limit to the number or specificity of "types" as Hirsch defines them.

The same principle of repeatability (and hence sharability) underlies Hirsch's notion of "intrinsic genre" (not to be confused with genre of the traditional literary sort). Here, however, Hirsch attempts to apply the principle of "intention" (as he understands it) to language. Chapter three ("The Concept of Genre") begins with a quotation from Wittgenstein,[11] part of which runs as follows:

> There are *countless* . . . different kinds of use of what we call "signs," "words," "sentences." And this multiplicity is not something fixed, given once and for all, but new types of language, new language-games, as we may say, come into existence, and others become obsolete and get forgotten [p. 68].

Hirsch supports his notion of genre at the level of individual utterances by appealing to Saussure's distinction between *langue* and *parole*. *Langue* is the set of rules and conventions that structure the potentiality of utterances. *Parole* is, at least according to Hirsch, also a set of norms: "the norms that do control and define the utterance, not the vast, uncertain array that could do so" (p. 70). "All understanding of verbal meaning is necessarily genre-bound" (p. 76). *Parole* is usually understood as a particular linguistic utterance, as opposed to the system of rules that govern utterances and make them possible. Although it may not be quite accurate to say that each and every *parole,* as Saussure defines it, is a set of actual (as opposed to potential) norms, Hirsch is probably right to point out that in any particular utterance certain rules and conventions are brought into play. However individualistic a particular utterance might be, if it is comprehensible, the principles that structure its meaning are (at least in theory) determinable: the utterance is therefore repeatable and thus sharable. It is the set of actualized rules and conventions applying to any specific utterance which is, according to Hirsch, that utterance's "intrinsic genre." Thus, although meaning is not "prejudiced" by its intrinsic genre, meaning does, in the course of its linear (textual) adumbration, have to be self-fulfilling. The intrinsic genre "is that sense of the whole by means of which an interpreter can correctly understand any part in its determinacy" (p. 86). Hirsch attempts to solve the paradox of the hermeneutic circle by suggesting that not only each portion of the text but the text itself in its entirety is a part of a whole (like the visible sides of a box), something which aims at a meaning, a complete intentional object. Interpretation thus simultaneously is objective (determinate) and goes beyond the semantic autonomy of the text itself.

Phenomenological Bracketing
versus Hermeneutic Circle

The Aims of Interpretation (1976) shows even more than Hirsch's earlier work the extent to which the meaning/significance distinction is the central tenet of his theory of interpretation. Having dealt with "meaning" in *Validity in Interpretation,* Hirsch had originally planned, he says, to devote the subsequent book to a consideration of "significance" and its relation to evaluation.[12] Instead, because of further speculation on the subject of "meaning," the later book is divided equally between the two concerns. "The unifying theme that binds these two parts together is the defense of the possibility of knowledge in interpretation."

This theme represents a substantial shift in emphasis from Hirsch's earlier book. He is now not so much concerned to defend the author

against the doctrine of "semantic autonomy" and the relativism it en-
genders; instead, he now wants to defend "the stable determinacy of
meaning" against what he terms "cognitive atheism" and what might
also be called, since the principal proponent of this view Hirsch takes to
be Jacques Derrida, "deconstructive" criticism.

In the pithy second section of chapter five, Hirsch tells us how *The
Aims of Interpretation* develops further the distinction between meaning
and significance. It becomes clear that, in shifting the focus of his
argument to meet head-on the challenge of deconstructionism, he has
come to defend meaning as such:

> This earlier discussion [in *Validity in Interpretation*] I now regard
> as being only a special application of a conception that is in
> principle universal. For the distinction between meaning and
> significance (and the clarifications it provides) are not limited to
> instances where meaning is equated with the author's original
> meaning; it holds as well for any and all instances of "anachronistic
> meaning" [p. 79].

This is an enormous shift in stance. One can only speculate about its
motivation, but two factors seem to be involved: 1) the deconstructive
attack on the possibility of any sort of meaning as such forces Hirsch to
withdraw his own depreciation of merely-interpreted meaning in order
to address the larger issue of the literary-critical enterprise itself; 2)
Hirsch has evidently come to believe, as it appears from the paragraph
quoted above, that the author's will must itself be an interpretive
construction and, hence, that interpretation, not intention, is the basic,
meaning-producing act. He still feels that we have an "ethical" imperative to respect the author's intention (p. 7), but it is one which "claims no
privileged sanction from metaphysics or analysis" (p. 90). Meaning is
"the determinate representation of a text for an interpreter" (p. 79).

Hirsch identifies two lines of development in post-Kantian phenomenology (pp. 4–6): that represented by Husserl and Frege and that
represented by Husserl's student Heidegger and carried on today by
"Heidegger's disciple Jacques Derrida" (p. 13). Hirsch relates these two
strains to what he sees as the central models upon which they are based.
Husserl posited a characteristic of consciousness to which he gave the
name, borrowing from Brentano, of "intentionality," the characteristic
of being conscious *of* something in a particular mode of givenness that
the mind is able to "bracket" or set off for contemplation. When such
bracketing occurs, we can observe the stability of mental contents over

the course of successive mental acts. The demarcation between intentionality and "the rest of our experience," says Hirsch, corresponds to that between "meaning" and "significance" (p. 5). According to Hirsch, Heidegger's objection to Husserl's view is an existential one: an "abstract cognitive model" does not live up to the fullness of experience. In place of bracketing, Heidegger adopts "the hermeneutic circle as expounded by Dilthey." Because "we must know the whole in a general way *before* we know a part, since the nature of the part as such is determined by its function in the larger whole" and "we can only know a whole through its parts, the process of interpretation is a circle." Hirsch regards it as a *vicious* circle.

> What we know at any time is "pre-conceptually" known and constituted by the whole of our world, and since that world changes in time, so must the objects (for us) change which that world preconstitutes [p. 5].

According to this view, "it is impossible to bracket off one part of experience," because each part is determined by the rest. Thus, while Husserl's model allows for objective stability, the implications of Heidegger's are relativistic.

Hirsch prefers the Husserlian model, partly because it helps to explain how meaning can be objectively sharable.

> The brackets implied by the terms "meaning" and "significance" do in fact represent something that most of us believe we experience in verbal discourse, namely, an alien meaning, something meant by an implied author or speaker who is not ourselves. Whenever we have posited another person's meaning, we have bracketed a region of our own experience as being that of another person [p. 6].

Hirsch finds this "paradox of self and other in verbal discourse . . . easier to accept" than that arising from the hermeneutic circle.

In fact, argues Hirsch at the end of chapter two, the hermeneutic circle is breakable. Developing the "positive" view of "pre-understanding" presented in *Validity in Interpretation* (Appendix II, Section E), Hirsch now attempts to explain the part-whole relationship in terms of Piaget's notion of "*corrigible schemata.*"

> Unlike one's unalterable and inescapable pre-understanding in Heidegger's account of the hermeneutic circle, a schema can be radically altered and corrected. A schema sets up a range of

predictions or expectations, which if fulfilled confirms the schema, but if not fulfilled causes us to revise it [p. 32].

Hirsch points out that expectation or "pre-understanding" can lead just as well to misinterpretations, at least before being revised. The key point, however, is that although a sense of the whole necessarily provides the background for our understanding of individual parts, this whole can *change* to accommodate and in turn stimulate the understanding of parts which do not seem to fit it. To be more accurate, one interpretive horizon may at any time, depending on the explicit foreground, be replaced with another. For the purpose of my investigation, however, even if we accept Hirsch's account of the interpretive act, the following questions remain to be answered. To what extent does Hirsch's shift to a defense of interpretation change his position in the debate about intention? How does this shift affect his crucial denial of a distinctly literary mode of meaning? To what extent does Hirsch's insistence on the objectivity of interpretive discourse as a carrier of meaning implicate him in what I have called the "interpretive fallacy"? Some consideration of another recent theory of interpretation may help us answer these important questions.

Juhl's Theory of Meaning as
Construed Authorial Intention

Peter D. Juhl has recently set forth an extended treatment of the relationship between intention and interpretation that differs from Hirsch's primarily in being more radical in its claims.[13] Juhl lists three "claims to be defended" in his introduction (pp. 12–15), and each of them points to a particular way in which Juhl has varied Hirsch's basic theory.

1. Juhl maintains that "there is a logical connection between statements about the meaning of a literary work and statements about the author's intention such that a statement about the meaning of a work *is* a statement about the author's intention." Whereas Hirsch had argued, in view of the possibility of multiple interpretations, the *ethical* demand to opt for the author's own interpretation, Juhl argues that to interpret a text is "necessarily" to "ascertain the author's intention."

2. Juhl states categorically—and here is the major exception to his otherwise general agreement with Hirsch—that our interpretation of

literary works "is determined not by our picture of the so-called implied author, but rather by our picture of the real, historical person." Even in *Validity in Interpretation* Hirsch had argued that all meaning implies an author which might be the interpreter himself; by the time of *The Aims of Interpretation,* Hirsch has come to the conclusion that authorial intention is an interpretive construct (however legitimate).

3. As we saw, it was the very possibility of a plurality or "Babel" of interpretations that suggested to Hirsch the ethical imperative of author-ity. Juhl, on the contrary, argues "on behalf of the view that a literary work has one and only one correct interpretation." This assertion is based on the double claim "(a) that a literary work cannot have logically incompatible meanings and (b) that there is reason to believe that it is in principle possible to determine the correct interpretation of a work."

Juhl is concerned, not with what Hancher calls "programmatic" intention, but with "active" intention:

> I am using the term in the sense of an author's intention in writing a certain sequence of words—in the sense, that is, of what he meant by the words he used [p. 14].

Juhl sets forth two basic arguments in support of his first proposal (that there is a logical connection between authorial intention and interpretation). The first of them is, in effect, that meaning is equivalent to the author's intention (whatever we take that to be). For example, Juhl demonstrates very convincingly how it is possible for a speaker's statement about his intention to disambiguate his utterance (chapter three, section three). Juhl maintains that the original utterance both a) acquires a new, correct meaning (from the point of view of the interpreter) and b) remains the self-same identical utterance; hence, the utterance is first truly understood when it is disambiguated.

Like Hirsch, Juhl does not acknowledge a uniquely "literary" mode of meaning. Consequently, he dismisses out of hand the notion of "internal" evidence for literary meaning (which, as I tried to show in the previous chapter, only makes sense if such a mode is postulated). The fact that textual features require less conjecture than intentionalist hypotheses does not mean for Juhl that the former are more valid evidence of literary meaning; rather,

> textual features are evidence for a claim about the meaning of a work *in virtue of* the fact that they are evidence of the author's

intention; it follows that insofar as facts about the author's beliefs, values, concerns, and so on are evidence of his intention— irrespective of where they are revealed . . . they will be no less relevant than textual features [p. 88].

According to this view, conjectures about authorial intention are as "relevant" as the text itself. In order to drive home his point, Juhl undertakes to refute "aesthetic arguments" about the nature of literary meaning, that is, to refute the very principle upon which the doctrine of the "intentional fallacy" is based. Juhl discusses three basic "aesthetic" arguments. The first is the claim that

a particular interpretation is more likely to be correct than another interpretation of a given passage because on the former the passage is better, richer, more profound, and so on than on the latter [p. 114].

Hirsch argues that, whenever the "best" reading is chosen over the apparently intended meaning of a work, the role of authorship is simply taken over by the critic. Juhl, on the other hand, consistent with the general claims of his introduction, insists that evidence for the richness, profundity, and the like of a text is logically evidence for the author's intention of richness or profundity.

The second "aesthetic" argument Juhl addresses is that texts contain implications of which the author is unaware. Hirsch argues that implication is a legitimate part of the interpretive horizon, comparable to the hidden sides of a box that is nonetheless perceived as a whole. Juhl takes the example of the "aesthetic" interpretation of a Donne poem by Graham Hough: "No doubt, Donne was not thinking of all the associations Hough mentions, but surely they are the sort of thing Donne meant" (p. 132). Like Hirsch, Juhl interprets meanings of which the author is not aware as being nonetheless manifestations of author-ity; unlike Hirsch, however, Juhl does not think of these meanings as unconscious, but rather as conscious at a more general level: evidence of meaning is evidence of an intention which can embrace that meaning.

From the two arguments just discussed, it is clear that Juhl considers a specific work to be the most convincing body of evidence for the intention that work expresses. He does not deny the legitimacy of the "best" reading or of "implied" meanings; rather, he simply insists that we attribute what we interpret to the historical author. When we choose an interpretation of the text that conflicts with the author's expressed intention—and this is Juhl's final counterargument against the doctrine of the "aesthetic"—it is because we take the text as better evidence of the author's intention than the explicit statement.

Juhl's line of reasoning is an especially useful one to consider in connection with the arguments of Hirsch because, although the two views seem very similar, it soon becomes clear why Hirsch hesitates to commit himself to a position as radical as Juhl's. Juhl's intentionalism is so radical that ultimately, as the paragraph above suggests, his position becomes almost indistinguishable from that of the New Criticism. If all meaning means by virtue of expressing an intention, then intention is something which (as Wimsatt and Beardsley insist) can be deduced from meaning.

I have argued that the notion of the intentional fallacy, while it might appear no more than an insistence on the obvious—that works actually mean what they are imputed to mean—is actually based on the subtle observation that ordinarily meaning *is* merely imputed. This character-istic of "ordinary" meaning reappears in what Hirsch describes as the necessity of author-ity and, even more obviously, in Juhl's "logical connection" between statements about meaning and statements about authorial intention.[14] There seems to me no denying Juhl's conclusions if one proceeds, as he does, on the assumption that literary texts mean in an ordinary way. However, Juhl leaves out of account Wimsatt and Beardsley's implicit assumption that literary texts mean in a way differ-ent from the ordinary. I have argued that the "intentional fallacy" is a special case of the "interpretive fallacy": the assumption that secondary, interpretive texts are semantically equivalent to literary texts (in my view the former merely attribute meaning to the latter). If I am right, then a "logical" connection between "statements about" literary mean-ing and authorial intention is irrelevant to Wimsatt and Beardsley's claim for a distinctly literary meaning. In fact, precisely because state-ments about meaning and meaning itself are not the same thing (pre-cisely, in other words, because periphrastic statements, whether they concern meaning or intention, presuppose mutual equivalence), such a connection *always* obtains.

On the other hand, Juhl seems to accept the notion of operative meaning without really being aware of the consequences of that accep-tance for his argument. When he takes on anti-intentionalist (especially "aesthetic") arguments which point to the apparent contradiction of authorial and textual meaning, he is perfectly willing to accept the text as the greater authority for what the author "intends." Wimsatt and

Beardsley, it will be remembered, raise no objection to authorial intention so long as it is deduced from or implied in the operative meaning of the text. Whether or not Wimsatt and Beardsley are justified in assuming a distinctly literary mode of meaning, they consider the "implied author" (to use Booth's term) to be a part of that meaning (see chapter one). Thus, Juhl seems to oscillate between a position which does not engage Wimsatt and Beardsley's objection to imputed meaning and a position to which Wimsatt and Beardsley do not object.

Each of Juhl's three major claims has the same underlying assumptions (and the same problems) as the intentionalist argument of Jeremy Lane and others (see chapter one). In other words, Juhl is able to argue a logical connection between meaning and intention because of his implicit assumption that texts embody intentions and that interpretation involves (at least potentially) the construal of intention. He is able to argue that the real author is involved because of the basic fact that intentions of others (and others in general) are accessible only through acts of interpretation. Finally, he is able to argue for one and only one correct interpretation because, by virtue of implying an author, texts must necessarily convey their own author-ity. The problem, of course, is that the author implied may, although each interpreter construes only one, be different from one interpreter to the next.

Not only is Juhl's author an implied author; his intention is, as I have already observed, an "active" (rather than merely "programmatic") intention: "what he [the author] meant by the words he used" (p. 14). This definition commits Juhl to a view of the author as interpreter, one whose understanding of the text is privileged (but one who, if he is to authorize interpretation, must himself be interpreted). The very argument that lends this sort of intentionalism credence, namely, the identification of understanding with intention, tends to blur the difference between author and reader and hence to undermine the authority of the author as an actual historical person. What really distinguishes Juhl's notion of intention from the intention as a function of meaning espoused by Hirsch (or, for that matter, Wimsatt and Beardsley) is Juhl's irrepressible willingness to take the authority implied by the interpretation of meaning as the "real, historical person."

Juhl's second and third claims follow from his first. He takes for granted the epistemological continuity between expressions of intention and interpretation of meaning; hence, he is able to argue that the implied author *is* the historical author, or rather—the wording is revealing—that interpretation is determined by "our picture of" the "real, historical person." Once one has denied the distinction between what is historical and what is "pictured" in interpretation, one could just as legitimately argue that the historical author is a mere fiction.

Because the "real" author can obviously be only a single individual (Juhl seems to overlook the joint authorship of texts such as "The Intentional Fallacy" or even the highly edited plays of Shakespeare), Juhl seems to feel that we must choose from among the multiplicity of possible implied authors the one true one. If there is only one author (that is, only one authoritatively "active" interpreter), then there can be "one and only one correct interpretation" of the work, Juhl's third major claim. The singularity of authorship leads to the "logical incompatibility" of any two meanings; at the same time, the accessibility of author-ity makes it "in principle possible" to determine what the one correct meaning is. (Juhl does not say what we are to do if the author *intends* an ambiguous or multiple meaning.) In other words, Juhl seems to imply, we have no epistemological sanction for disagreeing, though how we are to avoid it is a problem he does not address. In fact, Juhl's argument is circular. Meaning is what the historical author intends, he insists, but whatever meaning interpretation yields is, ipso facto, what the author intends.

Two Views of Intention

The fact that Hirsch avoids falling into the trap Juhl sets for himself indicates that Hirsch's unwillingness to carry his intentionalism beyond a certain point is more than mere hedging and shows the true, albeit perhaps unintended, subtlety of his position. Hirsch remains the most formidable proponent of intentionalist argument IVa (see previous chapter): the view that "intention" is embodied in the text itself. As such, he neither goes back to a pre-Wimsatt-and-Beardsleyan psychologism nor appropriates their discovery that intention may be part of the operative meaning of the text for an intentionalist viewpoint—Juhl seems to do both. Rather, he presents a genuine third position, which stresses the feasibility of bridging the gap between "active" and "operative" intention—between what a text means for the author and what it means for the reader. I have already pointed out that intentionalist argument IVa does not, for Wimsatt and Beardsley, involve the "intentional fallacy," because they claim that literary texts actually mean what they are supposed to mean. There is a sense in which both

Hirsch and his two predecessors attempt to defend textual unity against the claims of information that René Wellek would have called "extrinsic." The two camps have, of course, different notions of what information fits into this category, but the differences have undoubtedly been exaggerated by Hirsch's polemical stance (directed in large part against parties other than Wimsatt and Beardsley) and by popular oversimplifications of both sides of the debate. I will argue that the use of both sorts of "extrinsic" information can be subsumed under what I have called the interpretive fallacy and that Hirsch's extensive elaboration of a category of the *intrinsic* in his concept of "meaning" provides a much-needed grounding for the notion of internality on which the notion of the intentional fallacy depends.

I have already said that the doctrine of the intentional fallacy implies a concept of literary discourse as a distinct mode of meaning. Hirsch, of course, rejects this notion outright. But, defined the way Wimsatt and Beardsley seem to (as logically prior to whatever might be said about it), "literary" meaning would seem to have affinities with what Hirsch calls "meaning" in general. Wimsatt and Beardsley never denied that meaning expresses an intention; they denied only that *claims about* that intention are sufficient proof of its expression. If the notion of "literariness" is for Wimsatt and Beardsley related to that of operative meaning, then, for Hirsch all discourse would have to be literary to the extent that all discourse exists first and foremost as "meaning" (that is perhaps why Hirsch does not find the concept of literariness very useful or even tenable). Hirsch's careful distinction between "meaning" and "significance" might arguably be viewed as an extension of the principle of the "intentional" and "affective" fallacies to all acts of communication. It is obvious that Hirsch disapproves of the latter fallacy in the form of whimsical interpretations. But what is his argument against the changing significance of a text for its author if not the identification of an intentional fallacy?

However, Hirsch's concept of the text itself seems to differ in at least one important respect from that of Wimsatt and Beardsley. Hirsch views the author's meaning as something aimed at by, rather than fully present in and only in the text; hence, the text is epistemologically on a par with any and all information that will serve as evidence for that meaning. The issue is not, then, whether or not the author may correctly interpret his own work; what matters is whether, according to the theory of meaning involved, that interpretation (or, more precisely, its formulation outside the text) is relevant. For Wimsatt and Beardsley, that formulation is irrelevant insofar as it is not the meaning itself but merely possible evidence for it; and to the extent that it *is* relevant, it is the manifestation of an active intention and thus not in any privileged way the author's. Because, for Hirsch, the text aims at the author's intention (as the visible sides of a box aim at the whole six-sided figure), it is itself merely evidence for the interpretation of meaning; hence, there is no reason to exclude from consideration anything else that provides still further evidence for the intended meaning.

However, it is very important to distinguish Husserl's concept of "intentionality" from Hirsch's use of that concept and especially from Hirsch's concept of "intention" (see *Validity in Interpretation*, p. 218n.). It is true that Husserl relates the meaning aimed at by phenomenology to the subject or "cogito"; indeed, according to the model of intentionality, the cogito *is* intentional experience. "Each *cogito*, each conscious process, we may also say, *'means' something or other.*"[15] The fact that consciousness is always consciousness *of something* (the definition of intentionality according to Husserl) means that intentions are, in a sense, their own contents. That is why intentions are inaccessible: for an intention to be itself a content it must itself be intended. But this new intention is, like the previous one, a pure content—it is not aware of itself because it is nothing but the awareness of something else (the first intention). Thus, the "natural attitude"—the intention of intentions in judgments of their spatiotemporal referentiality—substitutes one intention for another and at the same time covers its tracks.

Hirsch's use of phenomenology to ground his own kind of objectivism seems to be based on a misunderstanding of the notion of intentionality itself. Husserl describes intentional objects as unities of meaning within "a passing flow of 'multiplicities'" (p. 40). Hirsch seizes upon this description as supporting the view that different acts of consciousness (such as those of author and reader) can provide different modes of access to the same thing (*Validity in Interpretation*, p. 21).

However, it is not the case, from Husserl's point of view, that appearances aim at objects: this division between perception as a mode of access and objects which exist independently of that mode characterizes the natural attitude and, consequently, runs exactly counter to Husserl's theory. For appearances to be distinguishable from objects in the way Hirsch seems to imply, there would have to be something one perceives prior to the interpretation of intentional meanings. But Husserl's starting point is that, even in its most primitive form, consciousness is meaning-ful. Intentional meanings are the most basic level of consciousness because their nonexistence is, literally, unthinkable. Husserl's point is that intentions have a duration, an identity, throughout a multiplicity of appearances. This means that intentional "objects" are not revealed by concrete appearances; rather, what appears is the intentional object itself as it is meant. This difference may not seem very great, but it is what distinguishes Husserl's theory from the "classical" view of an external reality mediated for a subject by the perception and interpretation of undifferentiated sense data. Hirsch continually replaces the object-as-it-appears, which for Husserl *is* the intention, with the object-as-referred-to-by-its-appearance, that is, with the "natural" object.

The practical difference between Hirsch's version of intentionality and Husserl's can be illustrated by a simple example both use: the intention of a cube (a die for Husserl, a box for Hirsch). Here are some excerpts from Hirsch's explanation of Husserl:

> When I look at a box, then close my eyes, and then reopen them, I can perceive in this second view the identical box I saw before. Yet, although I perceive the same box, the two acts of seeing are distinctly different. The same sort of result is obtained when I alter my acts of seeing spatially. If I go to another side of the room or stand on a chair, what I actually "see" alters with my change in perspective, and yet I still "perceive" the identical box. . . . The examples are paradigmatic: All events of consciousness, not simply those involving visual perception and memory, are characterized by the mind's ability to make modally and temporally different *acts* of awareness refer to the same *object* of awareness [*Validity in Interpretation*, p. 217].

Hirsch is not talking about the constitution of individual intentional acts, but rather about the relation of separate acts of intention to a hypothetical third term, the natural object. This object seems for Hirsch to result from a judgment of the spatiotemporal existence of the contents of the intentions in question, that is, a judgment of the truth-value of the intentions as acts of ontological reference. Hirsch's "object" is self-identical only because he postulates an equivalence between different acts of intention. That this is the case can be seen from Hirsch's extension of the notion of self-identity to the problem of verbal utterances.

Husserl's analysis (in my brief exposition) makes the following points then: Verbal meaning, being an intentional object, is unchanging, that is, it may be reproduced by different intentional acts and remains self-identical through all these reproductions. Verbal meaning is the sharable content of the speaker's intentional object. Since this meaning is both unchanging and interpersonal, it may be reproduced by the mental acts of different persons [p. 219].

For this last point to be valid, "different persons" or different subjectivities would have to be distinguished apart from and prior to the act or acts which yield the intentional object. But, according to Husserl at least, subjectivity is something *implied by* intentionality. Hirsch wishes to establish the objectivity and determinacy of authorial intention, but, as far as Husserl's intentional model is concerned, interpretation can never be subjugated to the mental act of any subject, since the activity of that subject will be wholly inferred from the interpretation itself.

For Husserl, the intentional object is not a common denominator (or, to use Hirsch's term, "type") aimed at by different modes of appearance. On the contrary, the intentional object is immanent within (or, more properly, as) the modes of its appearing:

For example, if I take the perceiving of this die as the theme for my description, I see in pure reflection that "this" die is given continuously as an objective unity in a multiform and changeable multiplicity of manners of appearing, which belong determinately to it. These in their temporal flow, are not an incoherent sequence of subjective processes. Rather they flow away in the unity of a synthesis, such that in them "one and the same" is intended as appearing [p. 39].

What Husserl describes is not a multiplicity of intentions aiming at a single object, but rather a multiplicity of "manners of appearing" aimed at by a single intention. Not only is the intentional object given in its appearances, but it is given *only* in its appearances and is in its appearances only *as given*. In other words, whereas Hirsch imagines the perceptions of both a side and a corner as referring to a box, Husserl would speak of the intention of "a-side-of-a-box" or "a-corner-of-a-box." So far as an "identical" intentional content is concerned (a box), only one "intention" is involved. To the extent that distinct appearances are perceived, they themselves are what is "intended"; hence, at least two separate intentional objects are involved. Furthermore, although the intentional object has, according to Husserl, a "determinate structure" (that is, it is given in its entirety by virtue of an implied "horizon of reference"), this notion cannot be used to support Hirsch's notion of determinate meaning, because Husserl's "determinate structure" can change:

> For example: the die leaves open a great variety of things pertaining to the unseen faces; yet it is already "construed" in advance as a die, in particular as colored, rough, and the like, though each of these determinations always leaves further particulars open. This leaving open, prior to further determinings (which perhaps never take place), is a moment included in the given consciousness itself; it is precisely what makes up the "horizon." As contrasted with mere clarification by means of anticipative "imaginings," there takes place, by means of an actually continuing perception, a *fulfilling* further determination (*and perhaps determination as otherwise*)— *but with new horizons of openness* [pp. 44–45, the second emphasis is mine].

Consistent with Husserl's general belief in the primacy of intention, this passage shows that the determinate structure of a particular implied horizon could never determine the nature of an intentional act, because that structure is a product of whatever act has already been carried out. If subsequent investigation reveals the side of a box to be the base of a pyramid, then the "same" perception would belong to a new "determinate structure" with a new "horizon." What this means for Hirsch is that the theory of intentionality might demand (as do Wimsatt and Beardsley) that meaning be operative (that is, have some determinate structure or other). However, the concept of "intention" cannot be used to dictate the course of intentional synthesis. "Determinacy," in Husserl's sense, is a characteristic of syntheses which have already occurred. Likewise, the "determinacy" of an intentional object cannot be used to adjudicate between conflicting intentions or meanings, since each, to the extent that it is operative, is ipso facto determinate.

The Interpretation of Authority

When Hirsch defines meaning as both "that which is represented by a text" and "what the author meant" (*Validity in Interpretation*, p. 8), he raises (and begs) the central question of the relation of "active" and interpretive (or "operative") meaning. The concept of "active" intention, as I tried to show in the preceding chapter, does not rule out the possibility of distinguishing extrinsic or "intentionalistic" evidence of meaning from meaning itself. Furthermore, even if it were true beyond any doubt that variance in "significance" presupposes a substratum of invariable "meaning," as Hirsch argues is the case when authors change their minds about their works (pp. 7–9), we would not therefore necessarily have to accept the authority of the author in determining that meaning. Hirsch seems to think of the notion of the critic-as-author as a self-evident absurdity, but it is not at all clear why there may not be variance (whether its source is the interpreter or the author) at the level of "meaning" as well.[16] In any case, we are left with the difficulty of determining who the "real" author is, and, even if we could arrive at such a determination, that author would still be the author for some *interpreter*.[17]

If the "critic" who supplies the meaning of the text could be called the "author" of that meaning (*Validity in Interpretation*, p. 3), then presumably it would make as much sense to call any author a "reader." It would make sense, because the entity that Hirsch here calls the "author" is one that is implied by an act of interpretation. By identifying the "author" with the "meaning," Hirsch clearly shows himself to be working with a notion of the "implied author." Thus, the "danger" identified in Hirsch's assertion that "a word sequence means nothing in particular until somebody either means something by it or understands something from it" (the danger that without the author we might have chaos) is not a real one: since Hirsch is presumably addressing readers, not authors, somebody *always* "understands something," even when what is understood is the "somebody" who "means something" (the "implied author") and Hirsch argues convincingly that that too must always be the case.[18] The supposed predicament that without authority "the text can have no determinate or determinable meaning" (*Validity in Interpretation*, p. 5) is not real either, because it is tautological. To assume the existence of "*the* meaning of the text" distinct from interpretations (which have to correspond to it) is to assume author-ity itself. The absence of authority would, of course, prevent any interpretation from being author-itative. But that is not to say that meaning would not still be an interpretation.

Many would deny that a text, considered in itself, has no determinate or determinable meaning.[19] People disagree about that meaning, but then they would almost certainly disagree about what the author's true intentions are: if disagreement is pluralism, then we have pluralism either way. It is doubtful that I could be the "author" of the meaning I construe in any practical sense because for me to perceive my interpretation as my own and not one suggesting itself to me in the text, I would need already to have become aware of a meaning which does *not* seem idiosyncratic. In other words, I would need already to have relinquished "my" meaning in favor of one I perceive as being more determinate.

Wimsatt and Beardsley's alternative to authority is not pluralism, let alone chaos. On the contrary, they argue that textual meaning is highly determinate and, above all, stable, because it does not vacillate in the crosscurrents of new evidence or supposition about the author's conscious intentions or milieu. Beardsley writes, "One of the main themes of Hirsch's book is that interpretations can be 'genuine knowledge' (p. viii), that they can be true or false, well-confirmed ('validated') or disconfirmed. In this issue, I am completely on his side" (p. 172).

I have argued that Wimsatt and Beardsley fail to problematize adequately the relationship of text to interpretation; that, by admitting explication as an adequate expression of poetic meaning, they forfeit the right to exclude expressions of intention which, if I am right, must be seen to have the same status as claimants to semantic equivalence. Hirsch is certainly right to the extent that, if the poem is treated as evidence of meaning, anything which provides additional evidence for that meaning is relevant. Thus, I argued that the notion of the "intentional fallacy" (or, for that matter, the notion of the "affective fallacy," since that too is a problem that occurs in interpretive discourse) might, as two "false" paths of interpretation, be subsumed under what I have called the "interpretive fallacy." If Wimsatt and Beardsley are successful in identifying a form of intentional argument which is external to poetic meaning, Hirsch could be said to have overlooked the possibility that the subject matter of all interpretive discourse (including expressions or inferences of intention) would rightly fall into the category of what he calls "significance." "Significance" is the relationship of "meaning" to "anything imaginable," says Hirsch at one point (*Validity in Interpretation*, p. 8); Hirsch himself argues that, when an author's remarks seem to indicate that his meaning has "changed," it is the "significance" of that meaning for him which has changed (see chapter one, section B): why would the same not hold true for an author's attitude toward his meaning which did *not* change? Even more important in this respect is Hirsch's insistence that, in cases where the author seems unable to explicate his meaning, that is of little or no consequence for the meaning itself, since it is the explanation and not the meaning which is hampered: Hirsch implies that meaning and explication of meaning are quite different. Hence, although the author might be a legitimate (or even privileged) interpreter-recipient of his text's meaning, when he becomes an interpreter-advocate—and he is not accessible to other readers in any other form—he places himself in a relation to his own work which really pertains to the text's "significance."

If the reader's knowledge of the author's intention takes us into the realm of "significance," then Hirsch's urging of that knowledge as a practical necessity is not only based on a misconception, but actually self-defeating: the appeal to the author does not save the text from the reader's idiosyncrasies (a goal espoused by Wimsatt and Beardsley as well as Hirsch), it only privileges one sort of reader significance—the sort most explicitly rejected by the doctrine of the "intentional fallacy"— namely, *the significance of the text for the author as his text's reader.*

Hirsch's second line of argument (meaning as sharable intention) seems flatly to contradict the ethical imperative of the first. If intention is indeed sharable, that is, if the gap between "active" and "operative" intention can indeed be bridged, then an ethical imperative would not be necessary. However, this contradiction emerges only to the extent that one insists on a form of intention that is not mediated through interpretation. Although he perhaps tries too hard to make the theory fit his own model, Hirsch's introduction of Frege into the debate is extremely useful, not only because Frege provides a solid philosophical ground for a distinction between "meaning" and the relation of meaning to other things, but also because, like Husserl, he helps to explain how intention could be sharable.

Hirsch claims that the distinction between "meaning" and "significance" comes from Frege's distinction between *Sinn* and *Bedeutung* (p. 211). The concept of "meaning" is important to Hirsch primarily for two reasons: 1) it is logically prior to significance, that is, it is presupposed by its relation to anything else or by any construction put upon it; 2) it remains stable throughout the variance of its relations or "significances." The problem is that only the first of these qualities characterizes Frege's notion of *Sinn*. The second, according to Frege, is an attribute of *Bedeutung*. [20] *Bedeutung* depends on the relation of *Sinn* (or "meaning") to a referent, and several "meanings" can have the same "reference" (such as "Scott" and "the author of *Waverly*"). According to Frege, then, the entity which remains stable throughout various formulations is the *Bedeutung*—the supposed model for Hirsch's concept of "significance." (I have already pointed out Wimsatt's comment to the effect that this supposed equivalence of various formulations is what distinguishes ordinary discourse from poetry: it is the pursuit of their differences which leads to the New Critical emphasis on stylistics.)

Perhaps realizing that he is confusing the very things Frege wants to keep separate, Hirsch immediately goes on to state that a particular *Sinn* may also have several *Bedeutungen*. Frege does not, as Hirsch himself admits, actually say that, and, in fact, Hirsch's interpolation is flatly contradictory to the sense of Frege's distinction. It is not at all clear how a single "meaning" could have several "references." Hirsch gives the example of the sentence, "There is a unicorn in the garden." This sentence, prima facie false, might be "true," says Hirsch, in the imaginative world of a Thurber; in other words, "its relevance would have shifted." But this example is misleading: there either is or is not a reference; in other words, a truth-value (which, for Frege, is what characterizes a "reference") must be positive or negative. That is not a wide spectrum of "significances," especially when one considers that the truth-value is positive or negative with regard to a single referent. In fact, it is a common characteristic of the two most prominent qualities of literary language as Beardsley describes them in "The Concept of Literature,"[21] namely, figurativeness and fictionality, that truth-value plays no role or, at least, has been decided beforehand (as when fiction is understood as opposed to fact).[22] Indeed, it seems to me that the Thurber example is a classic case of a literary utterance that cannot unproblematically be classified as either true *or* false.

Another distinction which seems to become conflated in Hirsch's discussion of meaning is that implied in the notion of "pre-understanding" (pp. 258 ff.). If pre-understanding is equivalent to the interpretive horizon, that is, to the intentional object in its adumbrative entirety, then what is "understanding"? Hirsch seems to explain both meaning and the context which makes meaning possible in terms of the same structure of an interpretive horizon. In the introduction to his book we read:

> The divinatory moment [of interpretation] is unmethodical, intuitive, sympathetic; it is an imaginative guess without which nothing can begin. The second, or critical moment of interpretation *submits* the first moment to a "high intellectual standard" by testing it against all the relevant knowledge available [p. x, my emphasis].

Yet the words "critical," "submit," and "high intellectual standard" (presumably the reader's) make it tempting to think that the "second" moment in question focuses on "significance" rather than on "meaning" as the two senses are defined by Hirsch. To be sure, Hirsch goes on to say,

"The following pages are mainly concerned with the second moment in interpretation," and the following pages, as we know, are concerned primarily with "meaning." One is tempted to ask what it is that one "submits" to critical reflection if not "meaning" itself. Determinate meaning would seem to be, in the combined light of this introductory statement and Hirsch's definitions on page 3, the second of *three* terms, with "divinatory" vagueness excluded at one end and shifts of relevance at the other. Nonetheless, Hirsch claims to be working with a single binary opposition with the result that, depending on whether he wishes to emphasize logical priority or determinate self-identity, his concept of "meaning" shifts between the poles of the dichotomy he has established (just as it partakes of the characteristics of *Sinn* at one point and *Bedeutung* at another). If this "first moment" is, as it seems to be, a moment of pre-understanding, then the "second moment," insofar as it is taken for the "meaning" of the text rather than for one form of its "significance," is the moment of what I have called the "interpretive fallacy."

Hirsch's concepts of "type" and "intrinsic genre" are grounded in the notion of pre-understanding. Hirsch does not seem to realize that, when he shifts the hypothetical locus of meaning from what is interpreted to what precedes interpretation (thus transforming Gadamer's "prejudice" into pre-understanding) something has to be left over that succeeds the moment of reading. This oversight, together with his confusion, at a critical moment, of "meaning" and "significance" (in his discussion of Frege), leads Hirsch to take for granted that the ability to subsume more than one experience (the characteristic of a "type" or "intrinsic genre") is equivalent to the ability to represent more than one experience. In doing so, he deproblematizes (and so begs) the question at hand of how experiences are shared. Hirsch does not prove that the meaning determined by the intrinsic genre is determinant for anyone other than the individual interpreter. Thus, we might be left with a "Babel" of determinant interpretations, but a Babel nonetheless.

Hirsch suggests a way around this problem by locating intentional meaning in a metaphorical space between individual subjects. This move would have the advantage of eliminating the epistemological gap between "active" and "operative" intention, that is, between the author-as-interpreter and the interpreter of the author, by submitting both to a "supra-individualistic principle which enforces meaning":

> Given a particular intrinsic genre, both the speaker and the inter-
> preter come under the same constrictions and necessities. It is

precisely at this very particularized level that the proponents of "public norms" have their vindication [p. 93].

This method of bridging the gap between author and reader simply assumes (as does Jeremy Lane: see chapter one) that there are *only* interpreters, that the author (like the reader) is engaged in an act of discovery of meaning or (to the extent that it is a *self*-discovery) of intention. This being the case, what Hirsch goes on to say next contradicts the point he has just made:

> Their mistake lay not in thinking that there is a supra-individualistic principle which enforces meaning, but in believing that this principle is somehow automatically given to any "competent reader." It is the speaker who wills the particular intrinsic genre and, having done so, is constrained by its proprieties, but the interpreter can never be completely certain what that genre is and can never completely codify its properties in all their complexity [*Validity in Interpretation*, pp. 93–94].

It is hard to see how meaning can at the same time be enforced by a "supra-individualistic principle" and "willed" by someone who is subordinated to that principle. Since the author in question is a textually disclosed one, Hirsch does not get around the idea of the "competent reader"; he simply redefines the notion of competence as the ability to identify the intrinsic genre "willed" by the author.

The "author's meaning" must necessarily, if it is to be understood at all, also be the interpreter's, and—to that extent—the "critic's" meaning, disparaged by Hirsch, must inevitably take precedence. The crucial question, for Hirsch as well as for Wimsatt and Beardsley, is: what is to constitute valid evidence for interpretation? The argument that the meaning of the text, once it is established, should be attributed to the author, has little effect on how we answer that question. Hirsch seems, in his discussions of authority, to alternate between a defense of what Wimsatt calls the "advisory" function of expressions or inferences of intention (which he finds perfectly acceptable) and an appeal to the practical arbitration of authority, which would be, according to Hirsch's own understanding of "meaning," merely arbitrary.

Everything Hirsch urges in favor of the doctrine of authority supports the conviction that it is an implied author (to whom the text's meaning is logically prior or, at the very least, who is not prior to the text's operative meaning) which is being defended. That the author is "constrained" by the set of norms constituted by his intrinsic genre, that the interpretive horizon of his meaning may contain "implied" or "unconscious" elements of which he is unaware (*Validity in Interpretation*, chapter two, sections E and G), that the author's "intention" is sharable in the same way that knowledge of perceptual objects is (implying that author and reader are epistemologically on a par): all suggest that the "author" is himself or herself a product, rather than the determining will, of interpretation.

In shifting his ground from the problem of authority to the problem of interpretation (as he does in *The Aims of Interpretation*), Hirsch yields a lot of territory staunchly defended in his earlier book. Nonetheless, "meaning" (as a determinate, sharable entity) remains his object.

Hirsch argues convincingly that the hermeneutic circle is not a vicious one, but he is less persuasive when he insists that it can be "broken." In describing the circle, making use of Piaget's notion of "schema and correction" as a "validating, self-correcting process" (p. 34), Hirsch makes it a vicious circle once more. According to Heidegger's description of being "in" the circle, it is the insistence on avoiding the circle that makes it vicious in the first place.[23] Hirsch assumes that the schema is objectively validated by the correction, but there is no point of stable reference outside the circle to ground such an objectivity: whatever doubt assails the initial schema can be brought to bear on the correction, on the next turn of the circle as well. It might be that such a view escapes a *particular* "prejudice" or, even more interestingly, that texts themselves might project and so create new horizons of interpretation, but Hirsch does not explain why the old problem does not simply crop up again at this new level. Even once the schema is "corrected," we still have the question of validity. Heidegger seems to suggest that the problem is caused by the desire for an external measure of validity itself.

Even if the dialectical notion of schema and correction did "break" the hermeneutic circle, it would have to be at the expense of the "objectivity" of meaning, as Hirsch has argued it. In 1960 he argued that objectivity depends on the determination of the explicit horizon of meaning by the logically prior interpretive horizon. Allowing for the flow of determination now from what is explicitly given to the interpretive horizon yields the carefully argued "control" which the horizon is supposed to exercise and hence the "objectivity" of the meaning. However, this allowance does help to explain how genre could be "intrinsic," that is, self-determining: the proper interpretive horizon would, in Hirsch's view, be determined by what is explicitly given. But if the explicit horizon (the text itself) structures its own interpretive horizon,

Hirsch's argument against "semantic autonomy" would seem to go by the board.

According to the notion of *corrigible schemata*, says Hirsch, "all cognition is analogous to interpretation" (p. 32). If true, this argument might be conclusive for his defense of determinate meaning. If indeed meaning were identical to interpretation, then the objective ground of interpretation—the adequacy of interpretation to its object, meaning—would be practically assured. However, this objective determinacy cannot be extended to interpretation as itself a communicative activity without ignoring the distinction very important to Hirsch between the *subtilitas intelligendi* and the *subtilitas explicandi* (see *Validity in Interpretation*, chapter four, especially section A). Thus, while meaning is self-determining—it is, after all, whatever is understood—interpretation (in what Hirsch thinks of as the more accurate sense of *subtilitas explicandi*, p. 129) must meet the demand for validity.

Previously Hirsch had maintained that meaning is grounded in or prefigured by the context or "horizon" (see "Objective Interpretation," section A). Now (in the model of *corrigible schemata*) he seems to say that it is that horizon itself which is the object of understanding. In other words, pre-understanding is now equated with understanding, explicit text with implicit meaning, textual species with intrinsic genre, and so on, eliminating the distinctions involved. If meaning *is* already interpretation, then meaning cannot be a stable entity prior to interpretation, and so, once meaning is realized, interpretation is superfluous. If, on the other hand, interpretation is understood to *aim at* meaning, then interpretation has the same intentional (that is, adumbrative) function as the text itself: interpretation could not therefore be associated with the horizon which allows the text to be understood. Indeed, I argued in the previous chapter that interpretation *(subtilitas explicandi)* always claims to do what the text being interpreted does. Thus, although the notion of *corrigible schemata* provides a compelling account of how meaning is understood, it cannot be used to validate interpretation based on claims of semantic equivalence.

Despite the fact that Hirsch launches his account of validity in interpretation with an outright rejection of the doctrine of the "intentional fallacy," his theory is not, in any final sense, at odds with that of Wimsatt and Beardsley. Wimsatt and Beardsley insist that poems actually mean what they are rightfully taken to mean; Hirsch sets forth an eloquent account of how, without ceasing to be the acts of communication of authors, they do just that. If Wimsatt and Beardsley fail to realize that they cannot logically exclude expressions or inferences of intention without excluding much of what we would ordinarily call "interpretation," Hirsch fails to realize that he cannot argue the distinction between "meaning" and "significance" without arguing that "meaning" is distinct from at least a certain kind of evidence *for* that "meaning." Again, it is Wimsatt and Beardsley's distinction of *literary* meaning which forms the basis of their notion of the "intentional fallacy." Hirsch, assuming that there is no difference between ordinary and literary discourse, argues convincingly that what he calls "meaning" is operative in literary discourse. The question would be, to my mind, whether it is operative as well in "ordinary" discourse. For Frege, at least, "meaning" (*Sinn*) is subordinated in ordinary discourse to "reference" (*Bedeutung*). In fact, Frege notes that in literature this is not the case: there is *Sinn* but no *Bedeutung* (see my discussion of this theory in chapter four). Hirsch's "meaning" may similarly help to explain exactly what a distinctly "literary" mode of meaning might be, and it is that possibility I would like to consider next.

Literature versus Significance

I have tried to show that at several key points Hirsch attributes one of the qualities of "reference"—objective determinacy—to "meaning." This is itself probably attributable to Hirsch's insistence that "meaning" is determinate. What I perceive as his mistake is that he equates the determinacy of meaning with the objective referentializability of meaning in interpretive discourse, that is, with the possibility of providing a semantic equivalent for the interpreted text. If "ordinary" discourse (such as that used to explicate works of literature) is based on something like what Hirsch describes as "significance" (that is, the relation of meaning to "anything else," in this case to semantically equivalent expressions in a nexus of "reference"), to what extent could "meaning" give us a concept of internality that would *allow* for the distinction of a "literary" mode of discourse? I have shown that Wimsatt and Beardsley accept that ordinary discourse is interpreted by a determination of the author's intentions. Hirsch, denying that literature works differently, is (if we grant Wimsatt and Beardsley's view) ipso facto able to argue that the same criteria apply to literature. But what if, as Wimsatt and Beardsley argue, one of the definitive characteristics of literary discourse were that its meaning is at variance with conventional usage, that is, with what would ordinarily serve to establish the author's intention?[24] In the obliqueness of overtly metaphorical language or the fictionality of literary "mimesis" (to recall again Beardsley's two criteria) there are simply no such clear-cut guides. As Hirsch no less than Wittgenstein points out (to be sure, in a different context), the intrinsic genre brought into being by the author is *new*. Ordinary discourse is arguably ordinary precisely because it is familiar (its metaphors, as Nietzsche once put it, have become "powerless," "used-up," its fictions truths).[25] In practice, we tend to value less works of literature in which newness (whether of language or of idea) is not forthcoming.

A good deal of light is shed on this question by Hirsch's linking of his notion of the "verbal type" to metaphor:

> Every creation of a new type involves the same leap of the imagination that flashed in Picasso when he turned a toy car into the head of a baboon. To make such an analogy is not merely to equate two known types—baboon and car—but to create a new one—the car-baboon. It is, in other words, the process of metaphor [*Validity in Interpretation*, p. 105].

The need for this process, according to Hirsch, "confronts a speaker who has to respond verbally to a new type of situation that cannot be automatically subsumed under previous types of usage," a situation which might well be that of the implied author of a literary text. Although the text's meaning or "intention" must be construed, this meaning is one which is closely bound to the text itself, that is, to a convention established by that text in the particularity of its expression rather than to an already established convention for which a wide variety of "equivalent" expressions might serve, as in ordinary discourse.

Hirsch does not seem to me to succeed entirely in arguing the validity of authority, but he does provide an eloquent description of the nature (or one aspect of it) of literary discourse. There are, says Hirsch, two types of type: the "new" ("car-baboon") and the "known" ("car" or "baboon"). The latter are language games which, in Wittgenstein's words, have "become obsolete" and been "forgotten" (that is, it has been forgotten that they *are* games). If "car-baboon" is recognizable as a metaphor, "car" and "baboon" are no less so as "ordinary" expressions.[26]

Hirsch himself gives an example of this process at work. When the telephone was invented, a new verbal situation was created: what does one say when one picks up the receiver? "Hello" in this country means the same thing as "pronto" in Italy, namely, that one is ready to listen; but "hello," unlike "pronto,"

> was a salutation and to say "hello" in this new situation was to assimilate the telephone response to a salutation. Once that metaphorical leap had been made, however, the new usage ceased to be a salutation at all. A new genre had been created [p. 106].

One might ask if it were not rather the case that the new genre had almost immediately been *un*created. When the metaphorical or (to that extent) literary force of "hello," however faint, was operative, an act of "interpretation," however simple, was required. Now, "hello" has become a part of ordinary parlance, ordinary because its meaning no longer requires the same sort of interpretation, but simply a conventional response. The "intrinsic" genre has become an "extrinsic" one: the import of the expression is no longer bound up with the "meaning" of the expression itself (as salutation) but rather with the relation of that meaning to a situation (in which its "significance" is wholly intentional—"I am ready to listen").

The distinction between "meaning" and "significance" could thus be understood as providing a theoretical ground for distinguishing that entity whose existence is assumed by Wimsatt and Beardsley and denied by Hirsch himself: a uniquely literary mode of discourse. The "literary" mode might be (or might be associated with) "meaning." "Literary," used in this way, has of course as *its* referent something much broader than any list of titles or particular words or phrases: "literary" would clearly refer to a function of language, to a kind of overt "language-game." But a broader definition of the "literary" would have the advantage of avoiding some of the contradictions (which Hirsch is right to point to) that arise from more or less "canonical" definitions—circular definitions in terms of a particular body or works pronounced to be literary.

On the other hand, if Hirsch's arguments are worked through consistently, practically all interpretation must be seen as formulating the interpreter's understanding of a text's "significance" rather than its "meaning." "Intrinsic criticism" is a misnomer, says Hirsch,

> for criticism is always intrinsic to the particular subject matter within which some aspect of the text has been placed and is always extrinsic to textual meaning itself, insofar as the critic directs his attention to concepts and criteria which lie outside that meaning [p. 144].

If we grant this, then we must grant that interpretive texts are caught in the same bind: either they convey the meaning of the text (in which case they must be identical to or strictly synonymous with the texts themselves, which also, in Hirsch's view, aim *at* a meaning) or they convey some other meaning (in which case interpretation is "extrinsic"). They might have an "advisory" function (see chapter one) in the determination of meaning, but, in so doing, they would demonstrate clearly the distinction in question. The secondary texts we call explications or interpretations relate the meanings of literary texts to something else, and that something else is the hypothetical referent, the common denominator implied in interpretation's claim to semantic equivalence. The new type "car-baboon" is not reducible, says Hirsch, to either "car" or "baboon." Yet a poem in which the word "car" appears as the same metaphor will be typically interpreted by means of the word "baboon"; indeed, it would not be unusual to speak of "baboon" as the "meaning" of the metaphor. Even "car-baboon," Hirsch's name for Picasso's meaning, is in the mode of the "forgotten" language game: "car-baboon" is a juxtaposition rather than an intentional coalescence. "Interpretation" gives us "meaning," but the meaning it gives us is that of ordinary, critical discourse rather than that of literature.

Granting the authority urged by Hirsch in interpretation would lead us into the interpretive fallacy in yet another way. If the author's intention is authoritative and the author's intention was to write a poem, then, says Hirsch, we are obliged "to understand a poem as a poem."

> Until the nature and purposes of a text have been grasped, its meaning will remain inaccessible, because its meaning is precisely something willed, something purposed. If I *understand* a poem as a newspaper headline (assuming that it is not a newspaper headline poem), then I have simply misunderstood it [p. 149].

But the problem is, as Hirsch goes on to point out, that "agreement has never been reached as to what a poem is and what its implicit aims and purposes are." Surely it could be argued that, in some cases at least, critical explications of poetic meaning involve treating the poem as something other than a poem simply by virtue of the fact that they translate poetic into critical language (or, that distinction denied, figurative into literal, fictive into referential). We need only imagine the case of a poet who refuses to express his or her intentions or otherwise paraphrase or explain his poems, believing them to be the best or only valid form of expression. This would be especially likely in the case of certain types of modern poetry where a premium is placed on indirect expression or even outright obfuscation (so-called "obscure" poetry). If a poet's intention involves a belief in semantic autonomy, in the uniqueness of poetic expression, then an appeal to his or her authority to validate an interpretation in ordinary (that is, literal, referential) language would be self-defeating.

3

Stanley Fish:
The Reader as Author

A Note on Chronology

The debate between Wimsatt and Beardsley on the one hand and Hirsch on the other is, at least on the surface, one about the conflicting claims of the "author" and of the "text." In recent years, however, very persuasive arguments have been put forth on behalf of a third entity as the locus of meaning in interpretation: the reader. Reader-oriented theories might in turn be divided roughly into three groups: theories which view reading as the performance of a fixed score (early Fish, early Wolfgang Iser), theories which view the reader as a source of meaning independent of the text (Fish in 1970, Norman Holland), and theories which define the act of reading in such a way as to cut straight across the distinctions between text, author, and reader (recent Fish, recent Iser).[1]

Since the second group of these theories rules out the problem of authorial intention (as a question of competing claims of "text" and "author"), that category does not warrant further consideration here. The first kind of reader aesthetics tends to favor the "text," since it views "meaning" as the successful performance (or experience) of textual strategies. The affinity of this view with Wimsatt and Beardsley's "operative intention" seems evident. Such a view is essentially formalist and Fish is quite right to categorize it as an extension of "New Criticism."[2] The third category of reader-oriented theory described above is not properly concerned with the reader at all, since the reader is understood as a function of the act of reading (that is, of the interpretive constraints— the operative public conventions—brought to bear upon the text).

Fish's main contribution to the debate about authorial intention is to deny the presuppositions which, in his view, make the debate between formalist and intentionalist possible: the distinction between "intention" and "meaning" (or the "text itself"):

> intention is no more embodied "in" the text than are formal units; rather an intention, like a formal unit, is made when perceptual or interpretive closure is hazarded: it is verified by an interpretive act, and I would add, it is not verifiable in any other way [p. 164].

The problem of intention is, at least in the cases I have considered so far, ultimately a problem in the definition of literary meaning. Fish's case is no exception: his contribution to the debate is based on a theory which is at once the most radical version so far of the thesis that meaning *is* the inference of intention and the most radical version so far of the thesis that intention is not accessible other than through—or as—the meaning of the text. The statement above expresses the second thesis. The following one expresses the first:

> intention and understanding are two ends of a conventional act, each of which necessarily stipulates (includes, defines, specifies) the other. To construct the profile of the informed or at-home reader is at the same time to characterize the author's intention and vice versa [p. 161].

Like Hirsch and Juhl, Fish considers meaning as identical to the construal of intention. Yet his rationale for doing so is different. For him, intention and the text "itself" have equal status with relation to a third entity, which is the reader's experience:

> This, then, is my thesis: that the form of the reader's experience, formal units, and the structure of intention are one, that they come into view simultaneously, and that therefore the questions of priority and independence do not arise [p. 165].

They do not arise so far as these three things are concerned, at least, but that is because all three are dependent on something which does have priority: the prevailing conventions of interpretation.

Terming Wimsatt and Beardsley's doctrine of the "affective fallacy" the "affective fallacy fallacy" (pp. 42 ff.),[3] Fish embraces what is anathema not only to them but to Hirsch as well: the notion that the meaning of the text is identical to how it affects the reader. Wimsatt and Beardsley want to avoid the "confusion between the poem and its *results* (what it is and what it *does*)" (*The Verbal Icon*, p. 21). Hirsch sees the doctrine of the intentional fallacy as leading to a particularly invidious form of the affective fallacy. For Fish, however, a poem can be nothing other than what it does, because meaning is an "event." The only question that makes any sense is "the question, what does this word, phrase, sentence, paragraph, chapter, novel, play, poem, *do?*" (pp. 26–27).

Thus, in rejecting the doctrine of the "affective fallacy," Fish also rejects the doctrine of the "intentional fallacy" (which he calls the "intentional fallacy fallacy").[4] If there is no text apart from the experience of reading, it cannot matter whether that experience is sanctioned under the rubric of "the author" or "the words on the page"—both are equally products of interpretation. That does not mean, however, as Fish insists, that "intentional" evidence for meaning is as legitimate as any meaning can be. If I am right that the notion of the intentional fallacy hinges upon the notion of merely imputed meaning, then the term "intentional" (as Wimsatt and Beardsley understand it) might well be replaced with the term "evidential," "putative," or (in a legal sense) "circumstantial." Thus, as far as Fish is concerned, the decisive question would seem to be whether the meaning evidenced (as an "intention" or otherwise) is actually a part of the experience of reading. I will argue that the possibility, implied in his argument, that meaning might be evidenced by being experienced makes Fish's theory not totally antithetical to that of Wimsatt and Beardsley.

Effective Stylistics

Is There a Text in This Class? records the intellectual development over the last ten years that has led Fish from reader-aesthetics to what I will call, for lack of a better name, interpretationism. Fish is himself very critical of his earlier theory:

> In 1970 I was asking the question "Is the reader or the text the source of meaning?" and the entities presupposed by the question *were* the text and the reader whose independence and stability were thus assumed [p. 1].

Far from taking up the cause "on behalf of the reader and against the self-sufficiency of the text," Fish's answer to the question made the reader "into an extension of formalist principles, as his every operation is said to be strictly controlled by the features of the text" (p. 7).[5] The

reason for this inadequacy in his earlier view, says Fish, was his own
"unthinking acceptance of another formalist assumption, the assumption that subjectivity is an ever present danger and that any critical
procedure must include a mechanism for holding it in check" (p. 9). Fish
began to free himself from this prejudice when he conceived the reader
"in such a way as to eliminate the category of 'the subjective' altogether"
(p. 10). In fact, he says, he had been wrong to assume the existence of
text and reader as independent entities. Not only is "the stability and
integrity of the text" dependent upon the act of reading, but the reader
himself is a subject whose consciousness is "wholly informed by conventional notions": "the self is constituted, no less than the texts it constitutes in turn, by conventional ways of thinking" (p. 11).

> Or to put it another way, the entities that were once seen as
> competing for the right to constrain interpretation (text, reader,
> author) are now all seen to be the *products* of interpretation. A
> polemic that was mounted in the name of the reader and against
> the text has ended by the subsuming of both the text and reader
> under the larger category of interpretation [pp. 16–17].

It is an open question whether Fish's new outlook represents an aban-
donment of his reader-response theory or an attempt to make it more
consistent. I will try to argue, somewhat against Fish, the latter view.

Earlier printings of Fish's first chapter, "Literature in the Reader:
Affective Stylistics," began with the heading "Meaning as Event." For
some reason it is left out in the book, but change the "as" to an "is" and it
is as pithy a summary of the whole essay as one could imagine. Fish begins
by presenting us with a couple of short texts which, conveniently (as he
admits), seem to resist our efforts to find a neatly packaged meaning.[6] He
then proceeds to analyze them in such a way as to show just how much
goes on when we read and *try* to make sense of the passages.

> Underlying these two analyses is a method, rather simple in con-
> cept, but complex (or at least complicated) in execution. The
> concept is simply the rigorous and disinterested asking of the
> question, What does this word, phrase, sentence, paragraph, chap-
> ter, novel, play, poem, *do?* And the execution involves an analysis
> of the developing responses of the reader in relation to the words
> as they succeed one another in time [pp. 26–27].

Fish gives the following example from *Paradise Lost* (I, 355): "Nor did
they not perceive the evil plight." His point is, quite simply, that there

is a difference between this particular construction, this exact choice of words and the paraphrasable message which those words quite literally (as a linear, temporal structure) add up to. I think most literary critics would accept this distinction, whether or not they agree with Fish on other counts, namely, that the utterance "says nothing"; that the difference lies precisely in the manipulative effects of the double negative ("the suspension of the reader between the alternatives its syntax momentarily offers"); and that the fallen angels see their plight "physically" but "they are blind to the moral significance of their situation" (p. 25).

Many would even be willing to admit that the difference, whatever it is, is one of *style*, affective or otherwise. What is—or was—provocative in Fish's account is his insistence that the "affect" revealed by his method is not simply the effect but the very meaning of the analyzed sentence:

> It [the sentence] is no longer an object, a thing-in-itself, but an *event*, something that *happens* to, and with the participation of, the reader. And it is this event, this happening—all of it and not anything that could be said about it or any information one might take away from it—that is, I would argue, the *meaning* of the sentence [p. 25].

The sort of meaning Fish has in mind here is one that is specific to a particular formulation and hence cannot be rendered by any *other* expression (which is what paraphrase is).[7] Fish is not so far in this respect from W. K. Wimsatt's statement that "in a certain sense no two different words or different phrases ever mean fully the same." However, Fish does *not* agree with what Wimsatt says immediately afterward: "That is the literary sense" (*The Verbal Icon*, p. xii). For Fish, this principle—that meaning is to be identified with the uniqueness of a particular verbal formulation—applies to all discourse:

> It follows, then, that it is impossible to mean the same thing in two (or more) different ways, although we tend to think that it happens all the time. We do this by substituting for our immediate linguistic experience an interpretation or abstraction of it, in which "it" is inevitably compromised. . . . And as we progress in this forgetting, we become capable of believing that sentences as different as these [Fish cites Whitehead and Pater on the "same point," which happens to be the very point Fish is making] are equivalent in meaning [p. 32].[8]

Now we come to the part of his early theory that Fish is later most anxious to repudiate. In 1970 Fish saw the "developing responses of the reader" as occurring "within the regulating and organizing mechanism" of semantic and other competences "preexisting the actual verbal experience" in the form of a "backlog of language experiences which determines probability of choice and therefore of response" (pp. 45–46). Even the early Fish saw that "the objectivity of the text is an illusion, and moreover, a dangerous illusion, because it is so physically convincing" (p. 43). Yet his initial insistence that the reader's response is determined by an appeal to competence evinced by the text itself made him guilty, he says a decade later, of a typically formalist offense:[9] although he had taken up the cause of the reader against formalism, the reader "is made into an extension of formalist principles, as his every operation is said to be strictly controlled by the features of the text" (p. 7). In 1980 Fish concludes

> that formal units are always a function of the interpretive model one brings to bear (they are not "in the text"). . . . There are still formal patterns, but they do not lie innocently in the world; rather, they are themselves constituted by an interpretive act. . . . The relationship between interpretation and text is thus reversed: interpretive strategies are not put into execution after reading; they are the shape of reading . . . they give texts their shape, making them rather than, as is usually assumed, arising from them [p. 13].

Earlier, says Fish, he had tried to maintain two mutually exclusive points of view: meaning as response (to counter the assumptions of New Criticism) and the determinacy of response (to confront the specter of solipsism). Now—the view is first set forth in "Interpreting the *Variorum*" (1975)—he no longer holds the latter position. But that does not mean that the reader replaces the text as a center of authority. The strategies which determine response

> proceed not from him but from the interpretive community of which he is a member; they are, in effect, community property, and insofar as they at once enable and limit the operations of his consciousness, he is too [p. 14].

It seems clear that Fish does not really abandon the notion of authority; he simply places it at a level beyond the control, or even awareness, of the individual.[10] This model calls to mind Hirsch's discussion of "prejudice" and "pre-understanding" (see previous chapter). Certainly Fish argues that meaning is in some sense "pre-understood" (e.g., p. 296); consequently he encounters the problem of the hermeneutic circle, that is, the problem of priority, despite his claim to have transcended it. Just as Hirsch fixes the necessary sense of whole arbitrarily as the ground of an objective interpretation, so Fish presupposes such a fixity as the logical ground of the concept of interpretive community.

Interpretationism

The question that serves as the title for his book *Is There a Text in This Class?* is useful to Fish as a fortuitous example of language's inherent ambiguity. One of Fish's former students approaches one of Fish's colleagues on the first day of a new semester and asks, "Is there a text in this class?" The professor responds, "Yes, it's the *Norton Anthology of Literature.*" "No, no," replies the student, "I mean in this class do we believe in poems and things, or is it just us?"

According to Fish, the "framework of contemporary critical debate" provides only two ways of accounting for this misunderstanding:

> either there *is* a literal meaning of the utterance and we should be able to say what it is, or there are as many meanings as there are readers and no one of them is literal. But the answer provided by my little story is that the utterance has *two* literal meanings [pp. 305–306].

Fish's argument is, in effect, that each of the parties in his anecdote "hears" a different sentence.

Fish sets forth this argument in response to Meyer Abrams's charge that the "New Readers" (Derrida, Bloom, Fish) rely on the norms of language in order to deconstruct them and hence that "literal or normative meanings are overridden by the actions of willful interpreters" (p. 305). This charge is unfounded, says Fish, because the interpreters themselves, far from manipulating the frames of reference in which meanings occur, are manipulated by them. We are manipulated and so are incapable of willful or arbitrary acts, because interpretive constraints are applied prior to consciousness; in fact, they are the very structure of consciousness, the shape of perception itself. Indeed, "you" and "I" are ourselves products, rather than sources, of interpretation (pp. 332–35). That is why interpretation always has the appearance of objective truth or, rather, why it *is* objective truth, since (and here is the answer to Abrams) there is nothing to which we could compare it as mere appearance. That is, furthermore, why Fish is able to say that

> the general or metacritical belief (to which I am trying to persuade
> you in these lectures) does not in any way affect the belief or set of
> beliefs (about the nature of literature, the proper mode of critical
> inquiry, the forms of literary evidence, and so on) which yields the
> interpretation that seems to you (or me) to be inescapable and
> obvious [p. 359].

One may, of course, be aware that it is possible to change one's mind.
But seriously entertaining the notion that a belief is just that—a belief—
is proof that one has already changed one's mind. That is because
doubting is also "something that one does *within* a set of assumptions"
and they compose the new belief one holds (p. 360). Fish's own theory,
as he is the first to admit, is an example of such a belief—now being held
without any assurance against being possibly abandoned in the future.

How one comes to change one's mind is another matter and by far the
least adequately explained part of Fish's theory. Changing one's mind,
as he tells us in his last chapter, is not a matter of "demonstration" but
of "persuasion." It is not a matter of demonstration, because whatever
evidence might be mustered in support of an interpretation would itself
be a product of that interpretation. An interpretation must already
have been accepted before evidence for it can be perceived *as* such.

Obviously, in order for someone to be persuaded, he or she has to be
fitted out with a new set of interpretive assumptions. How this happens,
given the impossibility of any individual's rising above his or her assumptions, remains shrouded in mystery. At one point (p. 366) it is clear
that persuasion "occurs when one perspective dislodges another and
brings with it entities that have not before been available" (the case with
affective stylistics, interpretationism, or the famous Eskimo reading of
Faulkner's "A Rose for Emily," p. 346). In fact, in the space of one
paragraph (pp. 368–69) devoted to "the status of [his] own discourse,"
Fish goes from asserting that he has tried to persuade us to accept a new
set of "assumptions and presuppositions" to insisting that he could not
have done so without situating his argument within the context of those
with which we are already familiar. This would seem on the surface to
be a conflation of "demonstration" (within the framework of assumptions accepted as true) and "persuasion" to new assumptions, the two
things Fish wants to keep distinct. However, there is a way out, and
although he does not come right out and state it, it is consistent both
with his method and with his advice on how to get ahead in the profession
of literary criticism, namely, to take a view of persuasion as essentially

deconstructive, that is, as invoking and manipulating currently held assumptions in order to unhinge them.

If this is Fish's view, it has some weaknesses. First, deconstruction is only one game, as Fish would be the first to admit; that is, it takes place within a particular set of assumptions which by their very nature as assumptions have no privileged status. Deconstruction can only account for one particular instance of persuasion. But even if we grant that deconstruction is always involved in persuasion's breakdown of old assumptions, Fish does not provide us with any account of how new systems are structured.

How to See a Poem When You Recognize It

The implications of interpretationism for literary criticism are simple and yet far-reaching. Everything that Fish says about interpretation in general applies also, of course, to literary interpretation. As a matter of fact, the difference between literary and nonliterary (or ordinary) drops out of the picture altogether; it exists as a way of looking at things, but it is not Fish's way, because, as we have seen, he explodes the myth of the literal or ordinary as an absolute standard of measure. If the meaning of ordinary language already requires a high degree of interpretation, literature cannot be distinguished as nonliteral, figurative discourse which interpretation is called upon to elucidate. Fish responds to the common-sense notion that in literature there are two levels of meaning (what is said and what is meant) by arguing that the figurative, symbolic, or interpreted meaning of a literary text *is* its literal meaning. Fish insists that, within whatever interpretive assumptions are operative, the poem is heard or understood immediately (on the surface) *as* its "literary" meaning or interpretation (rather than as literal discourse upon which literary meaning is superimposed).[11]

How, then, do we recognize a poem when we see one? Poetry reading, says Fish, is facilitated by a particular interpretive system, and poems are the reality which that system both creates and makes obvious (pp. 326–27). What this means is that, first of all, *any* utterance, looked at with "poetry-seeing eyes," will become literary and, if looked at differently, unliterary. Fish gives the example of a homework assignment that his students, when appropriately prompted, could successfully interpret as if it were a sixteenth-century religious poem (pp. 322–25). At a less

global, but for that reason all the more threatening, level, Fish insists
that particular critical approaches will always be successful at finding
supporting evidence in particular poems for the simple reason that they
put it there. Fish's conclusion, typically, cuts two ways. What might
seem the rankest cynicism has another, positive side. If interpreters
create the poems they interpret, the result is, as Fish says toward the end
of the book, "a greatly enhanced sense of the importance of our activities" (p. 368). It would almost seem as if a creative power were being
ascribed to the critic which has traditionally been reserved for the poet.
This does not eliminate the role of the poet—the critic by implication
becomes the poet—but it does raise a question about how we are to view
those authors (and their intentions) who provide critics with their
artistic medium.

One implication of a deconstructive view of persuasion would be a
dialectical relationship between systems of interpretation, a relationship which, while it would eliminate some of Fish's problems, is not
considered by him.[12] Fish speaks of his early affective stylistics as an
attempt to maintain two mutually exclusive points of view at the same
time. To meet the charge of solipsism, he would plead the text as a
determinant of response; to counter the accusation of engaging in a
subtle form of New Criticism, he would insist on the reader as the locus
of meaning (p. 7). Surely the same can be said of Fish's more recent
endeavors.

> The answer this book gives to its title question is "there is and their
> isn't." There isn't a text in this or any other class if one means by
> text what E. D. Hirsch and others mean by it, "an entity which
> always remains the same from one moment to the next" (*Validity in
> Interpretation*, p. 46); but there is a text in this and every class if one
> means by text the structure of meanings that is obvious and
> inescapable from the perspective of whatever interpretive as-
> sumptions happen to be in force [p. vii].

But, if Fish has been at all persuasive, he has convinced us that it is
impossible to have both of these points of view at the same time. If one's
assumptions allow for a "text itself," then it is not possible to doubt it *as*
a "perspective." Insofar as we know the text is merely a perspective,
there is no operative sense in which its meaning is "obvious and ines-
capable." At no time are both views actually held by the same person—
especially since "person" is something constituted *by* a view; yet, without
their theoretical co-presence (without, for example, the possibility of

assuming the self-identity of his title sentence across its two "literal" interpretations), Fish has no theory.

It is, of course, possible to argue a third alternative: the fish-eye view from which both of these other perspectives are theoretically possible. That would, however, entail a belief in Fish's view as emanating from a position of privilege. He could not then insist (as he does on page 370) that the implications his argument has for literary criticism are "none whatsoever." But Fish is adamant on the point that there *is* no third position: there is always *only another* perspective whose metacritical status is contained within (and disappears with) the assumptions that make it up.

It is important to see then that, just as the creative role of the poet is preserved, so is the determinacy of textual meaning. The "trap" which gives Fish his title was set, he says, "not by the student but by the infinite capacity of language for being appropriated" (p. 305). This objectification of language does not strike me as being very much different from the objectification of the text or of the reader, except that language is perhaps less felicitously personified. The passive construction evades the question: who is doing the appropriating?

The same could be said of Fish's appeal to the authority of interpretive community. Like the textual features which, in 1970, Fish sees as determining the reader's response, the notion of interpretive community preserves the objectivity of meaning. But, like those features, the assumptions of any interpretive community must themselves be interpreted, and, if we are to believe Fish, their interpretation could never proceed without certain assumptions. Fish often refers to the interpretive community of literary criticism as a monolithic structure he calls "the institution." But the institution, if Fish's debate with Abrams or Hirsch is any indication, is at war with itself.

Fish is, finally, not consistent in his account of the relationship between community and individual. In theory, Fish insists that communities encompass individuals (as when Kathleen Raine and E. D. Hirsch take for granted, even in the act of disagreeing, the existence of Blake's poem and the criteria for acceptable procedure in arguing an interpretation). In practice, however, interpretive systems would seem to be something which individuals can slip into and out of or even manipulate to the end of persuading others (such as Raine's *or* Hirsch's particular interpretations of that poem or Fish's metacritical viewpoint). Accordingly, the individual is not necessarily caught in Fish's double bind according to which one can neither transcend nor doubt one's own perspective.[13] I would suggest that Fish's failure to provide an account of how new systems are structured is due in part to his failure to take into account the dialectic of one perspective with another in the history of beliefs, which, however illusory its "progress" might be, is surely, as much as any single system, constitutive of the individual consciousness.

Fish in the Phenomenological Tradition

Fish is largely silent about the philosophical backgrounds of his theory, but there are some striking parallels between his views and those of some of his predecessors. For example, when he speaks of doubting one's own perspective, Fish says

> This infinite regress could be halted only if one could stand free of any ground whatsoever, if the mind could divest itself of all prejudices and presuppositions and start, in the Cartesian manner, from scratch; but then of course you would have nothing to start *with* and anything with which you *did* start (even "I think, therefore I am") would be a prejudice or a presupposition [p. 360].

Edmund Husserl, writing around 1929, criticizes Descartes for not realizing just this.[14] By assuming the *ego cogito* (i.e., the subject-object distinction) Descartes failed, according to Husserl, in his project of doubting everything that could be doubted in order to base philosophy on apodictic or incontestable grounds (note that Fish attributes to this very assumption his own earlier failure to doubt formalism, p. 14). For Husserl, too, there is no neutral standpoint from which to judge a situation or even one's own ego as such, but that does not lead to an infinite regress. What is left when one doubts not only the reality of the object, but the a priori givenness of the subject, is the givenness of the object itself as pure content. Husserl's name (borrowed from Brentano) for this quality of consciousness always to be consciousness *of something* is "intentionality" (Second Meditation, sections 14 and 17). But why is the phenomenological ground beyond doubt (or, to put the question as Fish might, why is what Husserl aims at not simply another interpretation)? First, it is extremely important to understand Husserl's method of doubting. To doubt, in this sense, does not mean to disbelieve; it means to suspend the question of belief altogether:

> This universal depriving of acceptance, this "inhibiting" or "putting out of play" of all positions taken toward the already-given Objective

world and, in the first place, all existential positions (those concerning being, illusion, possible being, being likely, probable, etc.)—or, as it is also called, this "phenomenological epoché" and "parenthesizing" of the Objective world—therefore does not leave us confronting nothing. On the contrary we gain possession of something by it; and what we (or, to speak more precisely, what I, the one who is meditating) acquire by it is my pure living, with all the pure subjective processes making this up, and everything meant in them, *purely as* meant in them: the universe of "phenomena" [pp. 20–21].

"Parenthesizing" (*Einklammern* has also been translated as "bracketing," see chapter two) is an unfortunate term insofar as it implies that something is being added to or performed upon a preexisting objective experience. But, from a Husserlian point of view, that is putting the cart before the horse. Husserl is very clear on the point that *epoché* involves the *suspension* of an act precisely in order to return to a preexisting state of affairs: "The fundamental phenomenological method of transcendental epoché, because it leads back to this realm [the realm of "transcendental being" prior to "natural being"] is called transcendental-phenomenological reduction" (p. 21). "Transcendental being" is thus not only antecedent to objective truth but also antecedent to "doubt" in the sense of disbelief. When the "natural standpoint" is "bracketed,"

> I do *not* then *deny* this "world," as though I were a sophist, *I do not doubt that it is there* as though I were a sceptic; but I use the "phenomenological" epoché, which *completely bars* me *from using any judgment that concerns spatio-temporal existence (Dasein).* [15]

When the judgment that gives us "objective reality" and (by virtue of a concomitant treatment of experiential phenomena as *reference to* that reality) "truth" or "falsehood" is suspended, what is left is not "nothing"; on the contrary, everything remains, but in a philosophically new mode: "By epoché we affect a reduction to our pure meaning (cogito) and to the meant, *purely as meant*" (*Cartesian Meditations*, p. 56, my emphasis). Contrary to Fish's assumption that what precedes belief must be prior to any act of interpretation (and hence cannot *be,* or be thought, at all), what for Husserl precedes the act which gives us objective belief is itself already a "meaning."

> Each *cogito,* each conscious process, we may also say, *"means" something or other* and bears in itself, in this manner peculiar to the *meant,* its particular *cogitatum.* Each does this, moreover, in its own fashion.

The house-perception means a house—more precisely, as this individual house—and means it in the fashion peculiar to perception; a house-memory means a house in the fashion peculiar to memory; a house-phantasy, in the fashion peculiar to phantasy. A predicative judging about a house, which perhaps is "there" perceptually, means it in just the fashion peculiar to judging. . . . Conscious processes are also called *intentional;* but then the word intentionality signifies nothing else than this universal fundamental property of consciousness: to be consciousness *of* something; as a *cogito,* to bear within itself its *cogitatum* [p. 33].

Such a definition of "meaning" does, however, correspond to Fish's notion of "interpretation" when he equates it, as he often does, with the immediate experience of meaningful wholes, whether in perception or communication. Like Fish, Husserl does not posit anything given prior to this intentional "meaning." However, Husserl carefully distinguishes (as does the early Fish and as the more recent Fish does not) between this sort of primary interpretation and *the interpretation of interpretation,* that is, the relation of meaning to something else in a structure of reference which characterizes belief within the natural attitude.

If I am right in saying this, light is shed on the question of "pre-understanding" as discussed by Hirsch and (indirectly) by Fish. That "meaning" at its most primordial level is "given" suggests that it is not organized by consciousness but prior to what is later re-cognized to be "consciousness." At the same time, what this understanding is *prior* to could only be the objective knowledge of the objective subject. If "pre-understanding" is understood in terms of the fact that consciousness is always consciousness *of* something complete, "intentionality," then there is nothing paradoxical about the notion of "pre-understanding," except from the "natural" point of view.

A "predicative judging" as a particular "fashion" of meaning is not to be confused (as it is by Fish) with the "judgment that concerns spatiotemporal existence." Husserl does say that the

predicates [of "being and non-being" and "truth (correctness) and falsity"] are not given ipso facto as phenomenological data, when the subjective meaning processes, or correlatively the meant objects as meant, are given; yet they have their "phenomenological origin" [p. 56].

In other words, these predicates belong "not to objects simpliciter" but to the "objective sense," or, as Husserl puts it elsewhere, "the whole world, when one is in the phenomenological attitude, is not accepted as actuality, but only as an actuality-phenomenon" (p. 32). Consequently, the difference between objectivism and the objective sense as meant is twofold. First, the intentional acts involved are different ones by virtue of having different objects: a house in the latter case, a "house-perception" in the former.

> Natural reflection alters the previously naive subjective process quite essentially; this process loses its original mode, "straight-forward," by the very fact that reflection makes an object out of what was previously a subjective process but not objective [p. 34].

What is involved here is "a new intentional process, which, with its peculiarity of 'relating back to the earlier process,' is awareness . . . of just that earlier process itself." That brings us to the second difference, namely, that in the case of objectivism or the "natural attitude" there is a doubling-up of intentional acts, at least insofar as a single object (the house) is concerned. "Natural reflection" replaces the intention of the house with *the intention of* the intention of the house (as representing or referring to a real, independently existing, "objective" house). In this "interpretation of interpretation" (to make a necessary adjustment to Fish's terminology) something is lost (the house as intention) and something is gained (the house as object).

In fact, the development of Fish's thought over the last decade is neatly epitomized in the shift of his concept of "interpretation" from a secondary and destructive intellectualization (comparable to Husserl's "natural attitude") to immediate experience or understanding itself (comparable to Husserl's "naive subjective process" to be recaptured through phenomenological epoché). In 1970 interpretation is under-stood in opposition to "meaning as event":

> It is only when readers become literary critics and the passing of judgment takes precedence over the reading experience, that opinions begin to diverge. The act of interpretation is often so removed from the act of reading that the latter (in time the former) is hardly remembered [p. 52].

In his introduction, Fish himself calls attention to his early distinction between meaning-as-event and conventional meaning or "what we usually call interpretation" (p. 5) and goes on to say, "I was practicing a brand of criticism whose most distinctive claim was not to be criticism at all but a means of undoing the damage that follows in criticism's wake" (p. 6). In considering interpretation as a "response to a response" or "passing of judgment," Fish seems to echo Husserl's distinction between intentionality (like "meaning" for the Fish of 1970, a temporal event constituted by conscious acts) and the "natural attitude" or "objectivity" which obtains when experienced meaning is submitted to and replaced by judgments of ontological reference. Like Fish, Husserl sees this objective referentiality as obscuring the "true" meaning of experience. Fish is, of course, speaking of literary texts and not experience in general, but by 1980 this difference has disappeared in the all-encompassing concept of interpretation.[16]

Already by 1973 ("What Is Stylistics and Why Are They Saying Such Terrible Things About It?") Fish's use of the word "interpretation" has begun to shift toward the pole of immediate experience with which it had been contrasted three years earlier.

> In the first statement of the position (in "Literature in the Reader") interpretation is characterized as a second-level response that prevents us from recognizing the shape of our immediate experiences; but in this essay interpretation is identified with that experience when I declare that the reader's activities *are* interpretive [p. 9].

From this it is clear that Fish does not, as one might think, abandon the concept of "meaning as event" for the radically skeptical view that there are only critical objects of one kind or another (this is, in fact, the "caricature" of deconstructionism from which Fish wants to disassociate himself, p. 268). On the contrary, Fish comes to the realization that the meaning constituted by experience is essentially interpretive: in criticizing and abandoning his early view of experience as transparent to some independently existing reality, he actually moves closer to Husserlian phenomenology. But what about "second-level" responses? There is no indication that Fish has by 1980 stopped believing in them; they simply drop out of the picture, or, to be more accurate, they drop into the general concept of interpretation, which, as I tried to show earlier, depends on the conflation of experience and judgment.[17]

Interpretation: Meaning
versus Reference

If my characterization of Fish as a closet phenomenologist is a fair one—at least one other critic has come to a similar conclusion[18] —then it is plain that he makes two mistakes, two wrong turns which lead him inevitably down a false path. The first is the assumption that underlies so many of his critiques of an opposition between interpretive community and objectivity. Exploding this opposition—objectivity can always be shown to be a function of interpretive community—allows Fish to give the impression that he has exploded a variety of conventional distinctions based on this opposition (such as that between the figurative and the literal meaning of an utterance). But even though Fish must assume that his victims have this opposition in order to debunk them by taking it away again, it is not really available to anyone (not even Fish). The only operative opposition, as Fish himself would probably agree, is that between interpretive community and *objectivism*, that is, a *belief* in experience as truthfully referring to objective reality. In other words, if interpretation is understood to be roughly parallel to intentionality, then there is another mode of knowledge (denied by Fish in theory but exemplified by the practice of his many deconstructions) parallel to the "natural attitude."

Fish's second mistake is his implicit assumption that the two terms of the opposition between interpretive community and objectivity are the same thing. However, according to Husserl at least, the natural attitude actually transforms intentionality: objectivity may not be absolute, but that does not mean it is indistinguishable from intentionality. Proving that the natural attitude is based on error does not eliminate it as a category. All it takes for the natural attitude and its concomitant objectivity to be operative is for someone to assume it: that is what it is, an assumption. In fact, if the natural attitude results from the ascription of spatiotemporal existence to intentional contents and the resultant truth-value of intention as reference (as Husserl suggests), then a debunking of the natural attitude can take place only within the natural attitude itself:[19] a truth-value is a truth-value, whether positive or negative, and the entire question of truth-value derives from the "natural attitude" rather than from intentionality.

Take for example Fish's critique of ordinary language ("Normal Circumstances and Other Special Cases"). Fish argues convincingly for the view that idiosyncratic understandings of an utterance (a salacious construal of a sign—"Private Members Only"—on the door of the Johns Hopkins faculty club) or an event (Pat Kelly's born-again Christian faith that his string of home runs is the result of divine intervention) cannot be explained as the imposition of an interpretive system upon the utterance or the event as they really are. That is because, as Fish argues, everything is understood within some interpretive system, some context. But for that very reason, because we are always in some context, one—that one—will appear to be not a context at all.

But can we conclude from this, as Fish does, that all meanings, normal and idiosyncratic, are the same? Isn't there a difference between understanding or "intending" a meaning and believing that that meaning corresponds to objective truth?[20] Certainly I am capable of entertaining the notion that "private members only" *means* that only genitalia are admitted to the Johns Hopkins faculty club; that is, with a little effort I can hear that sense of the utterance immediately. Or say I believe that Pat Kelly hit those home runs only because of his desire to achieve independent-agent status and bargain for a higher salary. What is the status of *his* account? Although I do not subscribe to it, it would not be true to say that I do not understand it (as Fish seems sometimes to imply). Fish would probably respond (as he does on page 361):

> It is always possible to entertain beliefs and opinions other than one's own; but that is precisely how they will be seen, as beliefs and opinions *other than one's own*. . . .

Exactly, I would say: that is the difference. Kelly's story has the quality of a fable or (if Fish's description above can be taken as a working definition) a fiction. Thus, it seems to me that the conclusion to the passage just quoted is unwarranted: "and therefore as beliefs and opinions that are false, or mistaken, or partial, or immature, or absurd." There is a sense in which all literature (the figure of a simile in a poem or the characters in a novel) has the quality of meaning that is entertained without being believed. Thus, when Fish says that within the framework of current critical debate the question "Is there a text in this class?" can only be seen to have either a single literal meaning or as many meanings as there are readers (hence, no literal meaning), he overlooks at least one other possibility: that of a single meaning which is *not* literal. Surely, for many literary critics this is the most interesting (or at least the most plausible) alternative. Fish assumes as much when he launches his attack on nonliteral discourse in order to dispel the "myth" of the literary.

Literary meaning cannot be opposed to ordinary meaning, according to Fish, because there *is* no ordinary (i.e., noninterpreted) meaning. There are only meanings-in-context which appear (within their contexts) literal, that is, they appear as the immediate, surface meaning. In this sense (which is for Fish the only sense there is) the figurative, symbolic, or other "literary" meaning of a literary text that interpretation reveals to us *is* the literal meaning.[21] I detect a logical problem here: the fact that all ordinary meaning is in some sense figurative does not mean that all figurative meaning is ordinary.

Fish does not really argue that figurative meaning is literal; he simply says that that is the way it is. But in doing so, he ignores the fact that, whether or not the "literal" level of a literary text (e.g., the tenor of a metaphor) is indeed unambiguously and objectively literal, it is a peculiar characteristic of literary language that two meanings (vehicle and tenor, for example) are involved.[22] For example, when Ophelia describes Hamlet as "th' expectancy and rose of the fair state" (*Hamlet*, III, 1), her comparison has force only because "rose" already means something. At another level, her outburst is expressive—she is lamenting what she perceives as Hamlet's madness—only because her words are meaningful in their context. It is Shakespeare who is, after all, speaking (and his message may be in a very real sense "literal"), but it is Ophelia's meaning that is the language Shakespeare speaks with. Whether or not her meaning is perfectly unequivocal—it is not really, even from a conventional point of view, "literal"—it must be construed somehow *before* we can begin to interpret the significance of the play (or even this part of it).

Or consider one of Fish's examples. He argues that a typological reading of Milton's *Samson Agonistes,* a reading "in which Samson's story is seen in relationship to the life of Christ" (p. 272) such as that put forward by William Madsen,

> is not a figurative significance, one that is imposed on the text's literal level; rather it is built into the text as it is *immediately* seen by anyone who operates within Madsen's interpretive assumptions [p. 273].

We might easily accept that the allegorical meaning of Milton's play is in some sense more "literal" than the actions performed by its characters (since that is the meaning which is "true" rather than fictive). We might also accept that Madsen's interpretation is determined to some extent (or even entirely) by his own expectations. But is it true, as Fish seems to imply, that the play has no plot or characters or action? If Fish is right, then what I experience when I read or attend a performance of *Samson Agonistes* (assuming I belong to Madsen's interpretive community) is identical to what I understand when I read Madsen's book. This conclusion is absurd, but it follows logically from the assumption that there are no literary texts themselves, only interpretations of texts. Fish would probably tell me now that I've missed the point. What is in question here is only the interpretation of the play: within Madsen's assumptions, his interpretation is immediately and obviously correct and all others false. But that is just my point. Fish is not talking about the meaning of the play; he is talking about the meaning of the interpretation. He substitutes (apparently without realizing that he is doing so) the meaning of one text (Madsen's) for another (Milton's). In Husserlian (or early Fishean) terms, he substitutes for the meaning of the text a judgment, implying a truth-value, about its reference. He replaces meaning with "interpretation," understood in his 1970 sense of something antithetical to meaning as event, thereby committing the error he took pains at that time to expose.

The basis of Fish's critique of objectivism is thus itself essentially objectivist. Fish assumes that only the absolute objectivity of what is implied in such terms as "literal" or "ordinary" could ground the distinction between them and the "figurative," "fictive," or, broadly, "literary." He overlooks the possibility (though it is one his own theory would seem to support) that "literal" and "ordinary" simply refer to particular uses of language, uses that are *constitutive* of the objects (or referents) which they mediate. Fish would probably reply that, because these uses are not independent of interpretive conventions (though the conventions they *are* dependent on may change), these uses are not ontologically different from uses which are figurative or fictive. But implied in this observation—Fish makes similar ones throughout the book—is the assumption that literal and nonliteral uses of language are on an equal basis because what they communicate is equally false (or, at least, falsifiable). But to say that something is false is as much to make a judgment of truth-value (revealing an objectivist orientation) as to say that something is true. Fish himself comments, "One cannot term the standard story [i.e., the "objective" reality shared by an interpretive community] a pretense without implying that there is another story that is not" (p. 243). Yet he does just that when he insists that there is a "difference" between *his* interpretation-relative model and that of Ralph Rader because, "I am aware that my model is an interpretation of reality rather than an approximation of it" (p. 146).[23]

Indeed, the opposition in Fish is always between what is immediately given as true (meaning within an interpretive community) and what is, because it has been exposed *as* the product of an interpretive community, "false, or mistaken, or partial, or immature, or absurd" (p. 361).

That literature might be thought to belong to this second category is surprising, yet that is the concept of literature he works with (if only to reject it):[24]

> To characterize literature by, for example, fictivity is finally not at all different from characterizing it as a formal departure from normative speech. Both characterizations depend on the positivist assumption of an objective "brute fact" world and a language answerable to it on the one hand, and of an entity (literature) *with diminished responsibility to that world* on the other [p. 110, my emphasis].

Such a concept of fictivity is, finally, naive. The situation is, therefore, hardly helped by Fish's insistence that literary meaning *is* "literal," if by that he means "objectively true." As I pointed out earlier (in connection with Pat Kelly's story), it is possible to *understand* something without *believing* it. Now, I would argue that it is possible to not believe something without necessarily believing it to be false. It is simply not the case that we think of literature as a lie; rather, we "suspend our disbelief" (Coleridge) without suspending our comprehension as we continue to read.

What I am suggesting is that we might slice the pie in a different way. The operative distinction, at least where literature is concerned, is not between true and false, but between what is true *or* false, on the one hand, and meaning to which the criterion of truth-value is not applied, on the other. Fish's inability to see beyond the first distinction—what I have argued to be his objectivism—is clear from what I take to be a statement of his current position. In the prefatory note to "Facts and Fictions: A Reply to Ralph Rader" Fish writes:

> I was thus flirting with a relativism that would be removed only when the notion of interpretive communities, grounded in a bedrock of belief, allowed me to preserve the distinction between the fictional and the true by understanding it as a conventional or community-specific distinction rather than as one rooted in nature and eternity [p. 136].

What "removes" the relativism and "preserves" the distinction between the fictional and the true here is, it seems to me, only another kind of relativism, one based on the "conventional or community-specific" assumption that all distinctions are conventional and community-specific. Fish's turn above is actually the closing of a circle. Is "the distinction between the fictional and the true" contained within the distinction between interpretive community and "nature and eternity" or is the distinction between interpretive community and "nature and eternity" contained within the distinction between "the fictional and the true"? Fish does not answer this question (and it is perhaps unanswerable), but the possibility of asking it pulls the teeth from the predictable Fishean response to the argument I have been developing, namely, that my views are themselves products of interpretation. That is no doubt "true," but since my arguments, like those of Fish, are concerned with that very distinction (since they are metacritical), it will never be clear whether my arguments are explained by or explain his predictable criticism of it.

If I am right in thinking that Fish's use of the word "interpretation" obscures the difference between intentionality and objectivism, then there may be two kinds of interpretation and, hence, no obvious reason why one of them might not correspond to what we think of as the "literal" level in literary discourse. Literature might thus indeed be understood as exploiting and deviating from "ordinary language," that is, whatever conventional reference is in force when a particular context has been successfully evoked.[25] If an interpretive community is large enough for many of us to agree on what is conventional (as Fish says it is) then there is no reason why it could not be the peculiar task of literature—I realize this is as much a stipulative definition as a factual description—to deform or restructure conventional reference in order to prefigure new interpretive systems and create new meanings. This at least has been the argument—and Fish does not answer it—of critics such as Roman Jakobson or, more recently, Wolfgang Iser. Such a view, which would see the diachronic dialectic in persuasion, would do what Fish's theory cannot: provide an account of the creation and understanding of something new.

Conclusion: Fish's Circle

I have argued that the notion of the intentional (or interpretive) fallacy is untenable (and indeed insignificant) without a concept of a uniquely literary mode of meaning. Fish, like Hirsch, rejects such a concept (or rather he accepts it in such a way as to neutralize the distinction between it and the concept of a nonliterary or ordinary mode) but, again like Hirsch, his theory is predicated upon a difference which makes it possible to save that distinction. Fish might protest that it is already saved, in the sense that the presuppositions of a certain interpretive community will allow for it. I have been suggesting that it is the possibility of "ordinary discourse" which makes that or any other community possible in the first place and, hence, that the space which literary discourse would occupy is marked out in Fish's theory no less than in that of Hirsch. Exactly what occupies that space, and how, is the subject of the following chapter.

Fish's attempt to distinguish between the act of interpretation and the objectifications of text and author leads him ultimately to a questionable objectification of the reader in the form of the "interpretive community." He thus remains within the objectivist position he sets out to criticize in two ways: first, in the "objectivity" of knowledge within the community (which he insists is not relative); and second, in the abstract falsifiability of knowledge of communities in general. What is obscured in this abstraction is the history of acts of understanding which must precede not only the objective text and the author's intention but our knowledge of the objective interpretive community as well. There is, according to Fish's own view, no disinterested (or unsituated) knowledge of any such stable entity as "the interpretive community." One is tempted to say that only God (who, knowing everything, could presumably know things that are mutually exclusive) could have such knowledge or embrace such ecumenicalism (by virtue of which "truth" is distributed equally all around with such largesse) as that envisaged by Stanley Fish. And that status, Rupert Brooke's poem "Heaven" notwithstanding (in which little fish imagine God as a big fish), is one that not even Stanley Fish would claim.[26]

4

When Literature Is:
Dual Meaning versus
Equivalent Meaning

Nelson Goodman once titled an essay "When Is Art?"[1] in order to suggest that people who were searching for the answer to the question "what is art?" were asking the wrong question. Goodman argues that an art object is not a thing, inherently different from other things, but rather the result of regarding something in a particular way. In effect, my defense-cum-revision of the notion of the intentional fallacy amounts to a similar claim with respect to the specific case of literature. The literary-critical notion of the "text itself" is a heuristic metaphor. A text is not a thing—I am assuming that paper and ink are not what we mean by "text"—it is rather the result of understanding a verbal act of communication in one way or another. As Hirsch explicitly and Fish implicitly argue, meaning is of the nature of an "intention" (in the phenomenological sense). The question "when is literature?" is, therefore, related to the question of intention and should be rephrased as follows: when is a verbal intention a literary intention? The investigation I carried out in chapter one of this book suggests that we might (at least partially) answer that question by answering another: when is a verbal intention immune to the claim of other verbal intentions, which attempt to "interpret" the former, to have the same intentional object? In other words, under what circumstances and with what effects does, in the case of a specific utterance, the interpretive fallacy obtain? In this chapter I will propose at least one answer to that question.

Paul de Man exemplifies the general misunderstanding of Wimsatt

and Beardsley's thesis even as he puts his finger on the source of that
misunderstanding. De Man realizes that a "clarification of the notion of
'intent' is of great importance for an evaluation of American criticism":

> Wimsatt and Beardsley coined the expression "intentional fallacy"
> as far back as 1942 and this formula, better than any other,
> delimits the horizon within which this criticism has operated.[2]

But de Man notes the apparent contradiction between Wimsatt's admission that "the poem conceived as a thing . . . is an abstraction. . . . The
poem is an act" (a view compatible with intentionalism) and his contention
that "if we are to lay hold of the poetic act to comprehend and evaluate it,
and if it has to pass current as critical object, it be hypostatized" (*The
Verbal Icon*, p. xvii). Wimsatt's contention, claims de Man, "changes the
literary act into a literary object by the suppression of its intentional
character" (p. 25). Indeed, he continues:

> The particular failure of American formalism, which has not
> produced works of major magnitude, is due to its lack of awareness
> of the intentional structure of literary form [p. 27].

I have tried to show in the foregoing chapters that, whether or not de
Man is justified in speaking of "failure" above, the doctrine of the
intentional fallacy does indeed "delimit the horizon" of American formalism. But, for that very reason, American formalism cannot be
faulted for "lack of awareness of the intentional structure of literary
form." Indeed, Wimsatt and Beardsley's insistence on the operative
meaning of the text itself can be understood precisely as an insistence on
the intentional (i.e., cognitive) nature of literary communication. In the
passage just quoted, de Man fails to distinguish between the New
Critical and the phenomenological senses of the term "intention": to
reject the former is, I have argued, to embrace the latter. Far from
denying the author's act of communication, the doctrine of the intentional fallacy is rather an implicit argument about the *way* he communi-
cates whenever he chooses to communicate poetically.

In ordinary communication the speaker's programmatic intention is
what concerns the interpreter. It does not really matter whether the
utterance is "Bring water!" or "Look at that smoke!" if the message is that
the house is on fire; even incoherent mutterings would suffice, so long
as someone could figure out what they referred to. In this sense,
ordinary communication is referential: what counts is what the speaker
wants to say. Because the utterance is only a means to express the

(programmatic) intention, any information (i.e., intentionalist evidence of all kinds) may validly be used to clarify the utterance's meaning (in the conventional sense of that term). In other words, what counts in ordinary communication is, paradoxically, not what an utterance means but what the speaker imputes it to mean.

Wimsatt and Beardsley's notion of ordinary communication suggests that a simple view of American formalism as locating the essential poetic element in something other than what words mean would be mistaken. Wimsatt and Beardsley distinguish mere evidence of intention from intention which is actually manifest in the text itself; in doing so, they assume the possibility of meaning that is operative rather than merely imputed. However, given that ordinary meaning is imputed by definition, such a possibility presupposes a meaning of a different kind. Indeed, the distinction between external and internal evidence (between the mere intention of value or meaning in a text and the text itself) would not be tenable without a notion of a distinct, *literary* mode of meaning.[3] The meaning of the text itself, in ordinary communication, is already external in the sense that it is referential (it aims at something else). In order to have a working concept of the internal (without which the notion of the "text itself" would be meaningless), it must be possible to distinguish between an utterance and the intention it expresses and, by implication, between two utterances that express the same intention.

Indeed, Wimsatt and Beardsley suggest that, because in ordinary communication a referent is intended, it becomes possible for two or more utterances to have the same meaning. The "poetic sense" of an utterance, however, according to Wimsatt, is peculiar to that particular utterance itself. There has been a tendency among recent critics of New Criticism to regard what is peculiar to a particular utterance itself as necessarily limited to purely formal or stylistic elements—this is the basis of such attacks on formalism and stylistics as that of Stanley Fish. However, it has been overlooked that the literary difference, as the difference between operative and merely imputed meaning, is a logical and semantic one.

The nature of this literary mode—or, to be more precise, the nature of a literary response to an utterance—is characterized in *The Verbal Icon* by the term "dramatic."

> The same dramatic principle applies, of course, and even more pointedly [than to the "dramatic reader"] to the speaker, or

speakers, of a poem. . . . Both speaker and dramatic audience
are assimilated into the implicit structure of the poem's meaning.
At the fully cognitive level of appreciation we unite in our own
minds both speaker and audience. . . . The means-end situation
of style and content becomes, in the dramatic focus, itself a
terminal fact of structure [pp. xv–xvi].

The term "dramatic," like the term "style," might seem to beg the
question of a distinctively "poetic" mode of meaning, since both of the
former presuppose as much as they explain the latter. However, Wimsatt seems to understand "dramatic" less as a quality inherent in some
utterances than as a structural relation into which any utterance might
enter. This structural relation is constituted by an additional level of
reflection.

The actual reader of a poem is something like a reader over
another reader's shoulder; he reads through the dramatic reader,
the person to whom the full tone of the poem is addressed in the
fictional situation [p. xv].

One implication of this structural relation seems to be that the reader of
poetry has his attention directed, not to any ulterior purpose of the
message whose communication is dramatized before him or her, but to
the message itself.[4] This inference is supported in another place where
Wimsatt describes the difference between literary and nonliterary
meaning in terms of the message itself over against the information
communicated:

In a certain sense no two different words or different phrases ever
mean fully the same. That is the literary sense. But there are other
senses . . . in which different formulations can and do mean the
same [pp. xii–xiii].

"Style," far from referring merely to ornamentation or nonsemantic
elements of language (such as phonemic patterns), seems here to be
connected with the totality of the message regarded in a special "sense"
as self-referential. Indeed, the constitutive iconicity of the poetic object
(from which Wimsatt takes his title) seems to be based on such a
structural relation. An icon, Wimsatt tells us, "is used today by semeiotic
writers to refer to a verbal sign which *somehow* shares the properties of,
or resembles, the objects which it denotes" (p. x). If the verbal icon
resembles what it denotes, then it might be fair to say that what it
denotes is verbal, specifically a verbal act such as itself. Indeed, the

notion that literary utterances, instead of having external referents, refer to themselves (i.e., that they are themselves what is denoted) accords well with Wimsatt's concept of the "dramatic." When we read "over another reader's shoulder," our attention is drawn away from what the words mean to the fact and significance of their meaning it.

> "A poem should not mean but be." A poem can *be* only through its *meaning*—since its medium is words—yet it *is,* simply *is,* in the sense that we have no excuse for inquiring what part is intended or meant. . . . In this respect poetry differs from practical messages, which are successful if and only if we correctly infer the intention [pp. 4–5].

A poem *is,* not in a general descriptive sense, but exactly to the extent that we pay attention to the text itself rather than to some "meaning" or "intention" for which the text is one of several interchangeable and expendable receptacles. The added, external dimension of practical messages leads Wimsatt and Beardsley to describe them as "more abstract than poetry."

If in literature it is the act and structure of utterance which are in question, then clearly literary and nonliterary modes of the same utterance are presumed to have distinct objects of reference: the latter, that which the speaker intends to communicate to the listener (or writer to reader): the former, these speakers and listeners themselves as dramatic figures. Intention (or, for that matter, meaning of a conventional kind) is irrelevant to poetic meaning for the simple reason that poetic meaning is defined by Wimsatt and Beardsley in part as utterance, the intentions of which have not (yet) been inquired into. To go beyond the immediate "dramatic" situation is to enter upon the "intentional" or "affective" fallacies (depending on the direction of the inquiry) because it is tantamount to treating literary texts as nonliterary ones (and in this case the way texts are received determines the mode in which they operate).

In a later essay Beardsley is more explicit about what makes literary discourse distinct from ordinary discourse. "A literary work," he says, could be defined as "any discourse that is *either* an imitation (compound) illocutionary act *or* distinctly above the norm in the ratio of implicit to explicit meaning."[5] The first of these criteria is a much more precise (and less circular) version of Wimsatt's earlier insistence on the "dramatic" nature of poetic utterance and is also a convincing definition of fictive discourse. The second criterion is an extension of Wimsatt's earlier emphasis on metaphor, "the structure most characteristic of concentrated poetry" (*The Verbal Icon*, p. 79). However, Beardsley admits,

> Unless we can demonstrate some connection between the two
> concepts included in this disjunctive predicate, the definition will
> seem as arbitrary and capricious as would a definition of "broose"
> as "anything that is either a broom or a moose" [p. 37].

Beardsley's attempt, which he admits is less than adequate, to reconcile these characteristics is as follows: both define literary works as "forms of verbal play that set a discourse notably apart from pragmatic functions" and "help to make a discourse self-centered and opaque, an object of attention in its own right" (p. 38). This proposal raises as many questions as it answers since, without really relating the two characteristics directly, it forces us back to the central question of what a verbal icon *is*. However, Beardsley does remind us that, whatever unifying principle is involved (assuming that one is and that it can be found), it must be able to account for the operative (as opposed to putative) nature of literary discourse. If the principle cannot do this, then the doctrine of the intentional fallacy is itself fallacious.

Frege's theory of the distinction between "meaning" and "reference" (see chapter two) provides us with a concept that may both link the characteristics Beardsley identifies and meet the logical demand for a distinct, operative mode of literary meaning, a demand which is implicit in the notion of the intentional fallacy. There are times, says Frege, when our attention is directed specifically to "meaning." One instance is the case of meanings which have no reference and, Frege implies, are not even supposed to have any.

> The sentence "Odysseus was set ashore at Ithaca while sound
> asleep" obviously has a meaning. But since it is doubtful whether
> the name "Odysseus," occurring therein, refers to anything, it is
> also doubtful whether the whole sentence does.[6]

It is no doubt possible, Frege continues, to take the sentence as having a reference by assuming it to be either true or false. This, however, is an attitude which modern-day readers of Homer (at least) rarely take because the sentence is obviously not true and yet it is unlikely that a statement thought of as false would be found interesting at all. Indeed, Frege's example here suggests that, whatever else might be placed in the category of nonreferential "meaning," what we call "fiction" certainly would be.

Another instance where the "meaning" of words is in question occurs when "one wishes to talk about the words themselves or their sense."

This happens, for instance, when the words of another are quoted. One's own words then first designate words of the other speaker, and only the latter have their usual reference. We then have signs of signs. In writing, the words are in this case enclosed in quotation marks [p. 58].

Frege terms this use of language "indirect" speech in which "the indirect reference of a word is . . . its customary meaning" (p. 59).

Consider the case of a story (in this case, a *Novelle*) that begins with the sentence, "As Gregor Samsa woke up one morning from troubled dreams, he found himself transformed into a monstrous bug."[7] It is a commonplace of literary interpretation that utterances such as these, insofar as they refer, are not to be attributed to the author of the text in which they occur, but rather to the narrator or "speaker." (Since the narrator does not really exist, of course, no one is held accountable for the truth-value of the reference.) Put another way, there is an implied phrase of quotation, a "he [the narrator, speaker, or dramatic character] said," which frames every such utterance.[8] In Frege's terms, every fictional utterance is "indirect"; that is, our attention is directed to its "meaning." This is especially clear in narration which contains submerged quotation or has the quality of free indirect style, interior monologue, or stream-of-consciousness, or (even more overtly) whenever dialogue is actually quoted. Even in non-narrative presentations of dialogue, as for example on the stage, the utterances in question, says Frege, would be "representations" of utterances, that is, signs which have "only meaning" (p. 63n.). Indeed, Frege associates "meaning" quite explicitly with "aesthetic delight" (which the "striving for truth" causes us perpetually to "advance from"), and I would like to suggest that the primacy of "meaning" in literary texts is due precisely to their status as "indirect" discourse.[9]

Ordinarily, of course, indirect discourse is effected by the embedding of one direct reference within another. This second reference is not reduced to the level of meaning, but remains in the referential mode (the "he said" of a direct quote, for example). In the case of literature, however, this second reference—the act of quotation—is implicit. The author of a poem does not actually say that he is quoting the speaker of the poem. Narrators quote explicitly but are themselves quoted implicitly by the implied author. If this were not the case, we would have "reference" rather than "meaning" before us. Nonetheless, we know that indirect discourse is in question when we read literature—this is Wimsatt's point when he speaks of the "dramatic" nature of literary statement—even if only by convention. And, although what we might call the frame reference (the "he said") is suppressed, we know (again by convention at least) that the indirect discourse presented in literary texts is purposeful. One difference involved in knowing (or reading as though one knew) that the "reference" in question is not the speaker's explicit one (which has been reduced to the level of "meaning") but the author's implicit one (the suppressed "he said") is that the question "What does this utterance refer to?" is replaced in explication with the question "Why is this utterance being presented?" One does not assume that there "really was" a Gregor Samsa who became a bug (although one undoubtedly must understand, at least in some general way, what it would be to become a bug); rather, one assumes that "Kafka" (who may well be a product of this assumption) has some purpose in *saying* that Gregor Samsa became a bug. If a salt shaker falls off a table in "real life," the incident is not generally regarded as a part of a meaningful whole (although it could be, for example, by a paranoid or by someone who, like Stanley Fish's Pat Kelly, saw everything as part of a divine plan) but rather as fortuitous. If, however, a salt shaker falls off a table in a novel or on the stage, we expect the event to have a purpose, whether or not we know what that purpose is (indeed, it is here—in determining what the purpose is—that almost all the controversy surrounding interpretation and "authorial intention" enters in) and however trivial that purpose might be (for example, as precipitating a comment that contributes to the development of a character).

It is doubtful that we could understand the "meaning" of an utterance if we were incapable of understanding it as "reference," that Kafka's story could speak to us if we were unable to imagine how it would be if someone *did* become a bug. "Meaning" should not be thought of as an ineffable quality of style conceived on a purely formal basis. Frege uses the obvious difference between modes of presentation ("the morning star" as opposed to "the evening star") to make clear the distinction between "meaning" and "reference," but that does not necessarily imply that "meaning" is strictly a matter of the connotations of a particular formulation. "Meaning," in indirect discourse at least, could be understood simply as "reference," considered as act rather than as having a truth-value. "Meaning" could thus be conceived as "reference" that is self-referential—this is explicitly the case in direct quotation—or "iconic."[10]

Frege's distinction can help us to understand what appears to be a logical contradiction in the argument I have been developing. Wimsatt and Beardsley suggest that literature is (uniquely) what is actually said (or actually meant). At least the first of Beardsley's later criteria (implicitness) suggests that what is meant in literature is (uniquely) something other than what is actually said. At the risk of adding to the confusion, I would like to suggest that the contradiction disappears if we consider literary meaning as facilitated by the structure of one meaning standing for another meaning, or "dual meaning."[11] But first I would like to show how the concept of "dual meaning" can provide a link between implicitness and Beardsley's other criterion (fictiveness).

It is fairly easy to see how the structure of "dual meaning" characterizes figurative expression. One "meaning" standing for another "meaning" might serve as a definition of figurativeness. I say that another "meaning" (not "reference") is indicated for the reasons that follow. Earlier I discussed Hirsch's example of Picasso's use of a toy car for the head of a baboon (see chapter two). Suppose this substitution occurred in a verbal situation (for example, a poem). Conventionally, a metaphor (for that is what we would have) has two terms, a vehicle and a tenor. The vehicle is what is said (in this case, "car") and the tenor is what the vehicle stands for (the head of a baboon). It would not be at all unusual for a literary critic to speak of the baboon's head as the "meaning" (by which we may understand "reference") of the metaphor.

However, a close consideration of what is actually experienced in the understanding of such a metaphor, especially in the light of Frege's theory, will show that the above account is wrong. If "baboon's head" as reference were the primary purpose of the metaphor, then the poet might just as well have said "baboon's head," and yet we recognize immediately that, in such a case, the metaphor would be lost. If we consider either of the two terms "car" or "baboon's head" at the level of reference, it becomes clear that the metaphor cannot be identified with either one. Obviously "car" is not to be taken as reference, since "car" stands for "baboon's head." Yet "baboon's head" is not the reference of the metaphor either, since, if that were the case, the image of the car would serve no purpose. Finally, the statement "the baboon's head is a car" (whether explicit or implicit) cannot be taken as reference, except in a negative sense, since the truth-value of such a reference is patently negative. Evidently, then, the primary semantic force of a metaphor is to be found at the level of "meaning," at the level of the expression itself in which "car" and "baboon's head" are juxtaposed in an analogical relationship. In the metaphor the mode of presentation is all-important: "car" is the mode of presentation of "baboon's head," but the force of the metaphor is not "baboon's head" but rather "car-as-baboon's head."

But is the structure of dual meaning also characteristic of fictiveness, as Beardsley understands it? Whenever an author presents us with imitations of illocutionary acts, their ordinary purpose as functional illocutions is suspended; however, their meaning *as* illocutions, although not functional, is preserved, and a new purpose is involved (what Beardsley calls an "aesthetic intention").[12] Fictiveness is thus, at least in literature, an instance of "dual meaning."

Even if Beardsley's criteria can be unified in the general principle of "dual meaning," we are still left with the apparent contradiction in the notion that in literary texts (and only in literary texts) a simple, operative meaning is involved. What appears to be a contradiction, however, is due to the assumption that what Beardsley calls "implicit" meaning— in effect I have argued that this one of his categories subsumes the other (fictiveness)—is more complex than "explicit" or ordinary meaning; that, in the case of the former, something is added to the latter. But, if we accept Frege's account, just the reverse may be true. According to Frege, "reference" (which I take to be the characteristic mode of ordinary discourse) is more, not less, complex than "meaning."[13] Referring is something we can use "meaning" to do: "reference" is "meaning" plus a judgment of truth-value (a judgment which, because it presupposes a referent, weakens the force of the "meaning" by making it equivalent to other "meanings"). If literature functions at the level of "meaning," then we have a basis—a principle of exclusion—for distinguishing the text itself from statements about the text (a basis which seems to be lacking once we admit the intentional nature of "meaning"). Statements about the literary text claim to offer perspectives on the "same" verbal intention (on the poem's "meaning" in the vague, conventional use of that term). But, in doing so, such statements claim semantic equivalence with the text itself; in other words, they treat as "reference" that which functions (ideally) as "meaning."

Whenever we have "dual meaning," we have an example of what Frege calls "indirect" discourse. Using an expression that is metaphorical or fictive is not essentially different from quoting, since the utterance in question is not presented for its referential value but rather *as* an utterance. Another way of saying this is that the utterance in question is self-referential. However, the term self-referential requires a certain qualification. In a direct quote, the utterance quoted is itself the referent of the entire sentence. However, the utterance does not refer to itself; rather, it is embedded in a direct-discourse (hence referential) utterance and is the referent of that second, different utterance. In literary discourse, the second, referential utterance (the "he says") is suppressed: the embedded utterance is still presented for its value as "meaning" but, rather than being itself the referent of another utterance, "meaning" in literature is presented for some purpose (some "aesthetic intention") which may be as small as the descriptive vividness of a figure of speech or as large as the central theme of an epic or entire oeuvre, and which may not be referentializable in ordinary discourse at all.

If my account of the relation of the doctrine of the "intentional fallacy" to the concepts of "meaning," "double meaning," and "self-referentiality" is accurate, then what has appeared to be a debate between camps loyal to the author on the one hand and to purely formal aspects of the text on the other may be interpreted quite differently. No doubt Wimsatt and Beardsley at times invite misunderstanding, especially when they seem to speak of the "text itself" as though it could somehow be divorced from a communicating consciousness. Wimsatt readily admits that the notion of the text itself, as object rather than act, is a heuristic device. Today we would be more likely to call it a useful metaphor. It is also no doubt true that followers of the New Criticism carried to an extreme the formalistic implications of the doctrine of the intentional fallacy: Hirsch is right to point out that the seminal essay in which that doctrine is first set forth does not argue what it is generally assumed to argue, namely, "that what an author intended is irrelevant to the meaning of his text" (*Validity in Interpretation*, p. 12).

Indeed, it is in the context of that false assumption that Hirsch's defense of the author should be viewed. Denying the conclusiveness of critical arguments based on mere authority ultimately became, Hirsch seems to feel, the basis for denying the act of authorship and, with it, the stability and determinacy of meaning. The energy of Hirsch's reaction should not blind us to some basic similarities between his views and those of Wimsatt and Beardsley. Both camps undertake to defend what they consider to be the constitutive element of literature, the text itself (though they seem on the surface to disagree about the locus of the text). Wimsatt and Beardsley defend literary meaning against the vagaries of intentionalist speculation; Hirsch defends literary meaning against the vagaries of speculative interpretation. Since, as I tried to show in chapter one, the author's meaning can be (and, according to Wimsatt and Beardsley, should be) operative meaning, there is a clear area where the opposing views of the two camps overlap.

In the notion of "significance," Hirsch provides for the first time a clearly formulated principle of exclusion, without which (as in the semantic equivalence of ordinary discourse) there is no means of distinguishing what is external to the text from what is the text itself. (One of Wimsatt and Beardsley's shortcomings is their failure to provide such a principle; indeed, not only are they mistaken to limit their critique to the particular case of the argument from authority, but insofar as they suggest that the text can itself be *evidence for* meaning they violate the doctrine of operative meaning.) Furthermore, in associating the phenomenological concept of "intention" with Frege's notion of "meaning," Hirsch provides the philosophical and linguistic ground for Wimsatt and Beardsley's paradoxical implication that ordinary meaning is not meaning at all. According to Frege, "reference" is based on a judgment of truth-value (namely, to amplify Frege in a somewhat Husserlian fashion, that of the existence of the referent). The relation of "meaning" to a referent allows for the possibility of semantic equivalence and, hence, for something akin to Hirsch's concept of "significance."

Hirsch argues that there can be a multiplicity of "references" related to a single "meaning" (see chapter two). These relations he calls "significances" of a particular "meaning." Frege, it will be remembered, says that a multiplicity of "meanings" can have a common "reference." Hirsch's rough and ready equation of "significance" with "reference" is therefore questionable. However, the fact that several "meanings" can have the same "reference" suggests that several "meanings" can, when they are judged as "references," be synonymous. Thus, although it is not correct to say that a single "meaning" can have several "references," it would be correct to say that a single "meaning" might have several referential equivalents. "Meaning" can therefore be distinguished from interpretive statements that claim synonymy with it, just as it can be distinguished from whatever reference it might be supposed to have. But such a distinction would encompass, not only the "significance" of "meaning" for its author, but any explication of his or her meaning by him or her (statements of intention) or anyone else (interpretations).

Although Hirsch attacks the notion of semantic autonomy, he makes a pretty good case for the independence of "meaning" from claims *about* "meaning," including those which come from the author, and hence for the extended concept of the "intentional fallacy," which I have termed the "interpretive fallacy." However, Hirsch does not pick up on Frege's and Wimsatt's discovery that pure "meaning" is the exceptional case, that what counts in ordinary discourse is "reference." Although Hirsch argues that literary meaning is not qualitatively different from ordinary meaning—he does so for the purpose of saving literature from a critical method that places no constraints on interpretation—he fails to realize that the difference might have to do with the difference between "meaning" and "reference" itself.

Stanley Fish rejects the distinction that forms the basis of the two earlier theories. Wimsatt and Beardsley are wrong to reject statements or inferences of authorial intention as evidence for literary meaning, he argues, but not because the author's intentions are sharable; rather, it is because, not only authorial intention, but all meaning, including that of the poem itself, is always and necessarily putative. (This is so true, says Fish, that the distinction between putative and active intention falls apart, since active intentions themselves—even one's own—cannot be other than the products of interpretation.)

Like Hirsch, Fish commits what I have called the "interpretive fallacy"; that is, he overlooks the "distinction between the meaning of an interpretation and the construction of meaning to which the interpretation refers" (*Validity in Interpretation,* p. 129), lumping the two together in his monistic concept of "interpretation." However, the distinction he ignores is present in his own theory, even though he does not recognize it. The single alternative to belief within an interpretive community is, according to Fish, disbelief. Disbelief occurs whenever the act of interpretation becomes manifest as such, that is, whenever the meaning of the act of interpretation is substituted for the meaning to which the interpretation refers. For Fish, there is only one interpretation of interpretation: falsehood. In other words, we only achieve the distance required to recognize an interpretation as an interpretation when we have abandoned it. But Fish overlooks the possibility of interpreting interpretation as valid; indeed, according to Husserl (and Frege), we do so all the time. The distinction between "meaning" and "reference" is more than analogous to that between "understanding" and "belief": just as for Frege "reference" is based on truth-value, for Husserl the "natural attitude" (which corresponds to what Fish calls "belief") is based on the assumed truth of "intention" as reference to reality. Thus, there are at least two kinds of "interpretation": that involved in acts of understanding, which need not involve belief, and that involved in judgments about acts of understanding as correct or incorrect and hence as believable or unbelievable.

However, in his relentless exposure of the interpretive constraints underlying our philosophical and literary-critical "givens," Fish goes as far as anyone yet to show the intentional basis of all belief and to show how belief is, in essence, something we do with intention. As far as literary criticism is concerned, Fish's achievement is not only to make an airtight case for the notion of operative meaning but also to show how universal is its degeneration—I use the term descriptively, not pejoratively—into belief. Like Hirsch, Fish denies that literature means differently from ordinary discourse, but, also like Hirsch, he goes a long way toward explaining wherein that difference might lie. Fish denies the difference because, in a way perfectly consistent with the thinking of Frege or Hirsch, he sees "interpretation" (i.e., "meaning") as the basis of all discourse. But, again like Hirsch, Fish does not recognize that ordinary reference is a use we make of interpreted meaning. He does not realize that ordinary discourse is a special case of literature (in the broad sense) and that literary meaning is in no way dependent on the ultimate validity of ordinary meaning.

If I have attempted to defend American formalism, then it has only been at the price of sacrificing, or at least altering, the concept of formalism itself. The notion of literary discourse which I have been developing is wholly semantic and wholly intentional. Although what is "intrinsic" to the literary text is of utmost theoretical importance to the concept of literature itself, my defense is probably of no use to advocates of "intrinsic criticism." According to the notion of the "interpretive fallacy," criticism becomes a highly suspect activity, since (at least in practice) it involves the systematic corruption of exactly what makes literature literature. My arguments suggest that literature (in the sense of a function of language that transcends not only canons but possibly even texts) is something which is to be understood rather than explicated. No doubt explication (or what is often called "interpretation") can and often does facilitate understanding, but there is the ever-present danger that the meaning of the explication will be substituted for the meaning of the poem and that this meaning will be imputed rather than understood, that is, cognitively experienced. One can never say what meaning means without assuming semantic equivalence, that is, without treating as reference what is essentially nonreferential (and possibly, in literature's creative aspect, nonreferentializable). To make a statement such as the preceding one is simply to stress what is obvious: critical explications are not literature but rather specimens of ordinary discourse. Therein lies both their use and their uselessness. Everyone who has ever taught even a mildly difficult poem knows that explication (in the familiar mode of everyday discourse) is indispensable. And every sophomore in an introductory literature class has at some time had the unpleasant experience of being told (and expected to believe) that a poem had a meaning or value which he or she was simply unable to see. But some students at least know the experience of having had their eyes opened by the right observation at the right moment. Since "literature" is a conventionally constituted entity, reading literature is a learned skill and the purpose of explication should be to educate the aesthetic understanding, not gratify the rage for objective (or what appears to be objective) truth. The conflict of interpretations will cease to present us with a choice between mutually exclusive alternatives and apparently boundless ambiguity when it is recognized that interpretations, far from giving us the truth about literary meaning (which should be the job of the poem), are or should be truly "self-consuming artifacts."

NOTES

Introduction

1. Vol. 4 (1967), p. 198.
2. Vol. 23, No. 23 (February 17, 1982).

Chapter One

1. *The Verbal Icon* (Lexington: The Univ. of Kentucky Press, 1954), p. 3.
2. Wimsatt and Beardsley here quote Archibald MacLeish, "Ars Poetica," *Collected Poems 1917–1952* (Boston: Houghton Mifflin, 1952). MacLeish certainly does not intend for us to take him literally, as another passage from this poem makes clear: "A poem should be wordless/As the flight of birds."
3. Read a certain way, Coomaraswamy seems to be the one who argues for intrinsic criticism.
4. This "sameness" obtains, of course, only from the point of view of the nonliterary mode, where several texts may all convey the same "intention" (cf. Wimsatt, pp. xii and 5).
5. Because I hope to show that literariness is not only a prerequisite of but actually based upon the concept of the intentional fallacy, I will postpone my discussion of Wimsatt and Beardsley's notions of literary discourse and the problem of a distinctly literary discourse in general until I have concluded my investigation of the problem of authorial intention (see chapter four).
6. In *The Disciplines of Criticism,* Peter Demetz, Thomas Greene, and Lowry Nelson, Jr. (New Haven: Yale Univ. Press, 1968), p. 195. The essay was reprinted with the title "Genesis: An Argument Resumed" in *Day of the Leopards* (New Haven: Yale Univ. Press, 1976), pp. 11–39.
7. *Innocence and Experience: An Introduction to Blake* (New Haven: Yale Univ. Press, 1964), pp. 263–65.
8. It would seem that the distinction between poetic and nonpoetic (or nonliterary) discourse is inseparable from the question of evaluation, which helps to determine both which text will count *as* the "poem" and what the "correct" meaning of that poem must be.

9. See "The Geneva School," *The Critical Quarterly* 8 (4) 1966, pp. 305–321.

10. See, for example, *The Verbal Icon*, pp. xii–xiii.

11. This subject is discussed further in chapter two and chapter four.

12. For surveys of this discussion up to 1968, see Wimsatt (1968); Peter D. Juhl, "Intention and Literary Interpretation," *Deutsche Vierteljahrsschrift für Literaturwissenschaft und Geistesgeschichte* 45 (1971), p. 1 ff.; Rosemarie Maier, "The 'Intentional Fallacy' and the Logic of Literary Criticism," *College English* 32 (2) 1970–71, pp. 135–45, see especially her note 3 (bibliography).

13. "Intention and Contemporary Literary Theory," *The Journal of Aesthetics and Art Criticism* 38 (1979–80), pp. 263 and 274.

14. "The Iconolatric Fallacy: On the Limitations of the Internal Method of Criticism," *The Journal of Aesthetics and Art Criticism* 26 (Fall 1967), pp. 12–13.

15. Seidler uses the term "intentional" in a philosophical sense roughly equivalent to "having to do with awareness" and thus establishes the connection between plan and meaning by fiat. However, if the concept of poem (in the broad sense) is understood to transcend individual texts, then a poem certainly might include much of what is ordinarily understood by the term "authorial intention."

16. Juhl, p. 4. Juhl's argument has recently been updated and expanded into a book which I consider in some detail in the next chapter.

17. See "Some Problems of Interpretation" in Arthur F. Wright, ed., *Studies in Chinese Thought* (Chicago: Univ. of Chicago Press, 1953), p. 240.

18. See Monroe C. Beardsley, *Aesthetics: Problems in the Philosophy of Criticism* (New York: Harcourt, Brace, and World, 1958), pp. 122–28. For further discussion, see chapter four below.

19. *The Rhetoric of Fiction* (Chicago: Univ. of Chicago Press, 1961), pp. 74–75.

20. *The Implied Reader* (Baltimore: Johns Hopkins Univ. Press, 1974), passim. Originally published as *Der Implizite Leser* (Munich: W. Fink, 1972).

21. "Art and Aesthetic Experience," *The British Journal of Aesthetics* 15 (1975), pp. 33–34.

22. "Intentions: The Speaker and the Artist," ibid., p. 40.

23. E.g., Robert D. Hume, "Intention and the Intrinsic in Literature," *College English* 29 (1967–68), p. 359, or Rosemarie Maier (see note 10). Since this position is argued insistently by E. D. Hirsch, it is dealt with extensively in chapter two.

24. *Modern Language Notes* 87 (1972), pp. 829–35.

25. *Theory of Literature*, with Austin Warren (New York: Harcourt, Brace, 1949), p. 148.

26. This point seems to me one of the best arguments for the view that

Wimsatt and Beardsley should have included something like what I call the "interpretive fallacy" in their descriptions of "external" information. If it were not the case that all explicative texts are extrinsic, Hancher's argument would be conclusive. The only grounds for excluding the author's report or analysis of his poetic understanding (which is no less valid than anyone else's) is that such reports are a) not infallible and b) qualitatively different from poetic meaning. But this is true of the writings of any critic, not just the author's.

27. "His Master's Voice? The Questioning of Authority in Literature," in *The Modern English Novel: The Reader, The Writer, and the Work*, Gabriel Josipovici, ed. ([New York:] Harper and Row, 1976), p. 117.

28. "Authorial Intention," *The British Journal of Aesthetics* 13 (3 [Summer, 1973]), p. 229.

Chapter Two

1. The reference is to Wellek and Warren, chapter twelve.

2. *Validity in Interpretation* (New Haven: Yale Univ. Press, 1967), pp. 6–10.

3. In a short article called "Intention," published four years before "The Intentional Fallacy," Wimsatt and Beardsley had argued that authorial intention is neither available nor desirable as a criterion for judging the "success" of a work of literature. By the time of their 1946 article, "success" has come to mean successful integration within the poem itself, that is, by implication, within the poetic mode of meaning. The earlier article appears in Joseph T. Shipley, ed., *Dictionary of World Literature* (New York: Philosophical Library, 1942), pp. 326–29.

4. "Poetry" here, as in the previous chapter, should be understood broadly as "literature."

5. First published in *PMLA* (1960).

6. Translating these terms is difficult. Hirsch leaves them both in German and risks confusing the ideas themselves, because both can be rendered as "meaning." Max Black translates *Sinn* and *Bedeutung* as "sense" and "reference" (not "referent," which he feels would be fundamentally wrong) in *Translations from the Philosophical Writings of Gottlob Frege*, edited by Peter Geach and Max Black (Oxford: Basil Blackwell, 1952). In the third edition (1980) "reference" is changed to "meaning" because "even 'reference' suggests thoughts alien to" Frege (p. ix). Peter F. Strawson develops Frege's distinction in an essay, "On Referring," *Mind* 59 (1950), pp. 320–44, where the terms "meaning" and "referring" are used. I will follow Strawson's lead and use "meaning" for *Sinn* and "reference" for *Bedeutung:* this corresponds to Hirsch's use of the term "meaning" and so should avoid confusion.

7. There is some debate about where this idea originates. Traditionally, Husserl is thought to have gotten it from Frege. But it has also been argued that Frege got it from Husserl. See J. N. Mohanty, "Husserl and Frege: A New Look at Their Relationship," *Research in Phenomenology* 4 (1974).

8. Kurt Mueller-Vollmer points to the long tradition in hermeneutics (beginning with Boeckh) of the notion that it is possible and even necessary to "understand an author better than the author himself." Precisely because the interpreter does not have direct access to the author's intention, the interpreter must know the "rules of grammar and stylistics" (and by implication all the necessary conditions and contexts) with which the author wrote, rules of which the author himself or herself may not and need not be aware. Such a view of interpretation might seem to cast doubt on the validity of inferring the author's intention (since he or she does not know enough), unless we revise our notion of the author along the lines proposed by Jeremy Lane (see previous chapter). However, Mueller-Vollmer concludes, in a move which Hirsch would appreciate, that the obligation to understand the author himself a) points to the essential author-ity (the "otherness") of meaning, and b) necessitates going beyond the "customary intrinsic approach" to supplement what the author, in his perhaps unreflecting act of creation, actually puts down on the page. See "To Understand an Author Better than the Author Himself: On the Hermeneutics of the Unspoken," *Language and Style* 5 (1) 1971, pp. 43–52. Cf. August Boeckh, *Enzyklopädie und Methodologie der philologischen Wissenschaften* (Leipzig: Teubner Verlag, 1886).

9. Tübingen: Mohr, 1960; translated as *Truth and Method* (New York: Seabury, 1975). This is not the place for an extensive discussion of Gadamer's position, but it must be noted here that Hirsch does not present it accurately. In fact, Gadamer's notion of *Vorurteil* does not form the basis of a hermeneutics of suspicion, as Hirsch fears, but rather is the very possibility of successful communication between author and reader. *Vorurteil* is the shared (or intersubjective) tradition, ultimately language itself, that makes communication possible in the first place. See *Wahrheit und Methode*, p. 261 ff., and Gadamer's *Kleine Schriften*, published in English as *Philosophical Hermeneutics* (Berkeley: Univ. of California Press, 1976), pp. 9, 15–16, and passim.

10. This view is remarkably similar to that of Stanley Fish, whose theory I will take up in the next chapter.

11. The reference is to *Philosophische Untersuchungen* (I, 23). Translated (with German text) by G. E. M. Anscombe (Oxford: Basil Blackwell, 1953), p. 11.

12. *The Aims of Interpretation* (Chicago: The Univ. of Chicago Press, 1976), p. 1.

13. *Interpretation: An Essay in the Philosophy of Literary Criticism* (Princeton: Princeton Univ. Press, 1980).

14. It is interesting to note that Stanley Fish, who stands at a skeptical

extreme from Hirsch and Juhl, exploits this characteristic in his attempt to debunk the "intention" controversy altogether (see the next chapter).

15. Edmund Husserl, *Cartesian Meditations,* trans. Dorion Cairns (The Hague: Martinus Nijhof, 1977), p. 33. Originally written around 1929 as lecture notes, these essays appear as Volume I of *Husserliana* (Haag: Martinus Nijhof, 1950) with the German title *Cartesianische Meditationen.*

16. Speaking of Hirsch's preference of F. W. Bateson's "correct" interpretation of Wordsworth's "A Slumber Did My Spirit Seal" to Cleanth Brooks's "better" one (see *Validity in Interpretation,* pp. 181–82, 227–29, 239–40), Michael Hancher wonders what is to be done with "Brooks's unauthorized reading." Hancher argues that Hirsch's theory of validity leaves no place for the products of "an art of interpretation" which "is also desirable and practical" and ought to be able to "coexist peacefully with its brother science." See "The Science of Interpretation and the Art of Interpretation," *Modern Language Notes* 85 (1970), pp. 795–97.

A conclusion similar to Hancher's is reached by Michael Steig, who points out Hirsch's own admission of variance in meaning and shows that even the most "subjective" interpretations are still interpretations of *meaning* (in Hirsch's sense). See "The Intentional Phallus: Determining Verbal Meaning in Literature," *The Journal of Aesthetics and Art Criticism* 36 (1977), pp. 52–55.

17. The circularity of Hirsch's insistence that the interpreter's meaning be subordinated to the author's when the author's meaning must itself be interpreted is, as Donald G. Marshall points out, still present in *The Aims of Interpretation* (where Hirsch turns from the author to the interpreter as the mediator of meaning). See his review of that work in the *Philological Quarterly* 56 (1977), pp. 52–55.

18. I am in agreement with Raval (p. 264) that Hirsch does not succeed "in countering the anti-intentionalist position . . . because Hirsch's authorial intention does not entail a biographical person but rather a 'speaking subject,' not really distinguishable from the New Critical persona." (The reference is to *Validity in Interpretation,* p. 242.) The problem, of course, is that Hirsch does not recognize this persona *as* a persona.

Morse Peckham concludes that, because they too are known through their utterances which must be interpreted, authors outside the poem have the same status as those acknowledged by Wimsatt and Beardsley to be inside the poem (as "biographical inference"): "the author of any statement is always, from the point of view of the responder, a construct." See "The Intentional? Fallacy?," *New Orleans Review* 1 (1968/69), p. 124.

John Huntley comes to a similar conclusion in "A Practical Look at E. D. Hirsch's *Validity in Interpretation,"* *A Symposium on E. D. Hirsch's* Validity in Interpretation, *Genre* 3 (July 1968), p. 252. Cf. also David Hoy (commenting on the same passage as Peckham, above): Hirsch's "speaking subject" resembles Wimsatt and Beardsley's "'dramatic speaker' . . . which is also a function of the text itself." Hoy continues, "Hirsch's new intentionalism therefore seems identical with the old anti-intentionalism, except for a different and much more complicated vocabulary." See *The Critical Circle: Literature, History, and Philosophical Hermeneutics* (Berkeley: Univ. of California Press, 1978), p. 31.

19. Beardsley, for example, attempts to refute what he calls Hirsch's "identity thesis" (the idea that the meaning of a text *is* what its author meant in writing it) with three counterarguments: 1) there are meaningful texts which were not authored, 2) "the meaning of a text can change after its author has died," and 3) "a text can have meanings that its author is not aware of." See "Textual Meaning and Authorial Meaning," *Symposium,* pp. 174–77. This essay, revised and amplified, appears as the first chapter of *The Possibility of Criticism* (Detroit: Wayne State Univ. Press, 1970) with the title "The Authority of the Text."

20. See Frege, p. 57. My account of Hirsch's account of Frege in this and the following paragraphs is corroborated by Hoy, pp. 22–23.

21. See my discussion of this essay in chapter four.

22. Barbara Herrnstein Smith, for example, argues that the reference of a poem is "historically indeterminate," that is, its "meanings, to the extent that the poem is offered and taken as a fictive utterance, will be understood to be unfixable, unlocatable in the historical universe." See *On the Margins of Discourse* (Chicago: Univ. of Chicago Press, 1978), p. 140.

23. Hoy points out that "Heidegger maintains that such circularity underlies all understanding, and that the methodological ideal of scientific objectivism is merely derivative, appropriate only for a limited range of cognition" (p. 3). I have tried to suggest that it is inappropriate for literary "cognition." Hoy seems to agree, concluding that the meaning of a poem may be what it "shows" rather than (as Hirsch seems to feel) what it objectively "says" (p. 39).

24. Cf. Smith, referring to "literary texts" (but also to other forms of discourse which do not depend upon the category of the "literary"): "What I have been suggesting, however, is that there is a class of verbal structures to which the assumptions governing ordinary speech *cannot* be extended because the suspension of those assumptions is precisely what defines that class" (p. 136).

25. See Friedrich Nietzsche, "Über Wahrheit und Lüge im aussermoralischen Sinne," in *Friedrich Nietzsche: Werke in drei Bänden* (Munich: Carl Hanser Verlag, 1966), Vol. 3, pp. 314–15. (Nietzsche wrote this essay between 1870 and 1873.)

26. Willard Quine, in a symposium on metaphor, describes the metaphorical extension involved in every subsequent use (in language acquisition and thereafter) of a word or expression (even in the most "ordinary" situations). See "A Postscript on Metaphor," *Critical Inquiry* 5 (1978–79), pp. 161–62.

Such would be the use, it seems to me, of "car" in a poem to describe the head of a baboon.

Chapter Three

1. There are no doubt other approaches to reader-aesthetics and other reader-aestheticians besides those I have mentioned here. However, these three categories seem to cover the basic relationships of any reader-aesthetics to the problem of authorial intention.

2. Stanley Fish, *Is There a Text in This Class?* (Cambridge: Harvard Univ. Press, 1980), p. 7.

3. This idea is carried over into Fish's later theory (as I will show), even though he later abjures his "affective stylistics."

4. This phrase does not appear in Fish's book, but I have heard him use it while debating various points when he visited the University of Iowa in the spring of 1978. Indeed, the epithet is perfectly consistent with his entire theory.

5. I was unfortunately beaten to the pun in the title of this section by Eugene R. Kintgen in "Effective Stylistics," *Centrum* 2, No. 1 (1975), p. 43. Yet Kintgen pleads for a truly "effective" stylistics, whereas I allude to Fish's later conviction that the "affect" of the text is really an "effect" of the interpreter.

6. Norman Holland points out that "Fish's 'informed reader' concentrates on only one kind of emotion: doubt and the resolution of doubt." See "Stanley Fish, Stanley Fish," *Genre* 10 (3) 1977, p. 438. William Ray responds to Fish's comment that a particular sentence "has the advantage of not saying anything . . . you can't get a fact out of it" (p. 23) with the comment: "Assumed, of course, is that *facts* are what one reads for," which, Ray goes on to imply, is not necessarily the case, especially in literature. See "Supersession and the Subject: A Reconsideration of Stanley Fish's 'Affective Stylistics,'" *Diacritics* 8 (1978), pp. 64 ff.

7. Ralph Rader argues that Fish is not true to this precept: "Fish, in contrasting my emphasis on final meaning with his on the process of meaning-finding, seems in reconsidering the Sir Thomas Browne sentence to agree that, after the process of meaning-finding, a final meaning does appear. This admission . . . is inconsistent with his general position and clearly at odds with the thrust of his original analysis." See "Explaining Our Literary Understanding: A Response to Jay Schleusener and Stanley Fish," *Critical Inquiry* 1, No. 4 (1975), p. 910. Rader also points out that the notion of a determinate final meaning need not rule out a consideration of meaning as process. He compares the piano piece which one has learned well and can perform over and over again to "the frustrating succession of fumbling steps by which a pianist

learns to play a piece," which would be an analogy to Fish's view (p. 909).

8. This wonderful definition of ordinary discourse should be kept in mind when, as I will show below, Fish later denies any distinction between ordinary discourse and experienced meaning.

9. Holland criticizes Fish on the same count, but makes a point which Fish does not. Speaking of Fish's "stop-motion method of reading," Holland says that, "Fish offers a theory of reading in which the text's contribution and the reader's alternate in time," reading and hypothesizing alternating "until—touchdown!" Holland contrasts that view with his own, one which the later Fish (albeit with reservations about the status of the reader) would probably approve: "in a transactive model, the reader initiates the reading transaction, supplying at every moment his schemata for perception and interpretation to see what the text will give back through them" (p. 434).

10. Holland points out the danger of speaking of "the" or even "an" experience, since to do so suggests "that there can be an experience of a text somehow displaced or separated from the person doing the experiencing" (p. 436). Holland also points out a contradiction in Fish's reader-aesthetics: "Nothing is to be discarded from the *event* of reading, but one is to suppress large chunks of the *person* reading. In effect, Fish assumes the reader is a mystic writing pad: he starts life as a *tabula rasa*, gets scribbled all over by his own twentieth-century experience, but with a flip of the plastic surface, he can erase those idiosyncratic marks, respond to a poem or story in a professionally approved way, and the deeper grooves in the wax will have no effect on that response" (p. 437). Fish no doubt comes to share this view of his earlier theory to a certain extent, but Holland sees the problem as cropping up again in Fish's later theory: "Most recently, however, Fish has taken another tack: not defining the single reader, but an interpretive community, through which the single reader can limit himself to impersonal or transpersonal standards, another kind of erase-and-rewrite, yet one still directed to interpretation" (pp. 437–89).

11. This argument seems a logical outgrowth of what Ray describes as Fish's earlier equation of meaning with "propositional import," such that the act of reading is reduced to the search for an "easy referentiality." Hence, Ray's comment—"the single thing which one does *not* normally take a literary text for is precisely 'the report either of an existing state of affairs or of an act of interpretation'" (pp. 65–66)—seems applicable here as well.

12. Here one sees the enormous gulf that lies between Fish's relativism and the hermeneutics of Heidegger and Gadamer that Fish's position seems at times to resemble. Both Fish and Gadamer stress the historicity of the interpreter, but for Fish history is closed: one is either in an interpretive community or not; there is no dialectic *within* a community. Gadamer, on the other hand, conceives the process of history in terms of the dialectical nature of understanding within a community. He speaks of this dialectic variously as

a dialogue, a game, or a "fusion of horizons" that transforms the interpretive horizon of the reader and allows for the communication of something new, a point of major importance for Gadamer's student Wolfgang Iser. Fish fails to recognize that the encounter with the text might itself be a significant event in the reader's history or in the formation of an interpretive community. See Gadamer, *Philosophical Hermeneutics,* pp. 3–17.

13. If we discount the implication that he is speaking from a metacritical position where *everyone* is wrong, there is a sense of this dialectical view in Fish's observation: "The moral is not that no one can ever demonstrate to someone else that he is wrong but that the parties to a dispute must already be agreed as to what will count as a demonstration" (p. 295). After all, the level of community is limited by the number of members: at some point, at least in theory, a level would be reached where *everyone* agrees.

Rader claims (with some justification) to be a victim of Fish's manipulation for his own purposes of these levels of agreement: according to Rader, Fish's attack on Rader "operates under different explanatory standards from those he adopts elsewhere. The statement quoted imputes to my theory as a special defect the fact of its supposedly self-fulfilling and nonfalsifiable character, whereas Fish clearly asserts that all interpretations including his own are *necessarily* self-confirming" (p. 908). Fish seems to ignore his own declaration that "assumptions are not all held at the same level and that a challenge to one proceeds within the precinct of others that are, at least for the time being, exempt from challenge" (p. 296). Note that Fish describes this activity as "an act of persuasion," not of demonstration, suggesting that the process by which interpretive communities acquire members is carried out dialectically within a larger system of interacting communities.

14. *Cartesian Meditations,* First Meditation, Sections 10 and 11. See chapter two, note 16.

15. *Ideas,* trans. by W. K. Boyce Gibson (New York: Humanities Press, [1931]), pp. 110–11. Originally published in German as *Ideen zu einer reinen Phänomenologie und phänomenologische Philosophie,* Book One (Halle/Saale: Max Niemeyer, 1913).

16. In other words, Fish does not recognize an ontological distinction between language and reality, because he does not recognize the distinction between what must be interpreted and what simply is (the latter must be interpreted, too). Fish's attack on the doctrine of the "text itself" is carried at one point so far as to argue that even the objectivity of "letters, paper, graphite, black marks on white paper" is the result of interpretation (p. 331). Because for Fish reality is "interpretation" and because for Husserl intention is "meaning," I would say that they *are* playing in the same ball park, even though on the surface they seem to set forth an epistemology and a rhetoric, respectively. Fish's theory is a rhetoric because, for him, reality is a matter of persuasion. However, to the extent that the natural attitude is facilitated by

belief (or nonbelief, which amounts to the same thing), the same could be said of Husserl.

17. Cf. Ray: "the collection of interpretations [in "Affective Stylistics" and *Self-Consuming Artifacts*] in fact portrays the activities of two very distinct readers: one who goes through the motions of reading and is progressively illuminated, and one (Fish) who weighs the significance of that illumination—or the resistance to it—in terms of a generalized literary-historical context. The former indeed graduates from an outward, discursive type of cognition to an inner vision. But the latter is doomed to retranslate this immediate vision into a further outward discursive form, whose lack of immediacy or loss of Truth he can only compensate for by integrating it into the larger truth of the institutions of history and literature" (p. 68).

18. Cf. Ray: "this paradigm [Ray is speaking of *Self-Consuming Artifacts*] presents a fascinating parallel to that of the movement of reading as described by the phenomenological approach: progressively displacing a differentiated (linguistic) and fragmented order 'where everything is in its proper place,' with a harmonious unity in which all is co-present and interrelated, the reader gradually constitutes an inner vision, whose 'moment of full emergence is marked by the transformation of the visible and segmented world into an emblem of its creator's indwelling presence'" (p. 63). My argument is of course that the later Fish is still working within the bounds of a phenomenological critique of objectivism.

19. John Reichert points out that, in order for there to be two "normal," "ordinary," "objective" accounts of Pat Kelly's home runs (or we might add, two "literal" meanings of Fish's title sentence), there must be some thing or event which the two interpretations have in common; otherwise, there would be nothing to disagree upon. Another way of saying this is to observe that Fish, in the very act of denying any objective level prior to acts of interpretation, presupposes such a level as a logical necessity. "If Kelly and the reporter agree about nothing whatsoever, then of course there is nothing for them to disagree over." See "But That Was in Another Ball Park: A Reply to Stanley Fish," *Critical Inquiry* 6, No. 1 (1979), pp. 165–66.

20. Nelson Goodman, whose acceptance of many right worlds (as opposed to one right one or many relative ones) is remarkably similar to that of Fish, is nonetheless led to quite a different set of conclusions. "On these terms, knowing cannot be exclusively or even primarily a matter of determining what is true. . . . An increase in acuity of insight or in range of comprehension, rather than a change of belief, occurs when we find in a pictured forest a face we already knew was there, or learn to distinguish stylistic differences among works already classified by artist or composer or writer. . . . Such growth in knowledge is not by formation or fixation of belief but by the advancement of understanding." See *Ways of Worldmaking* (Indianapolis: Hackett Publishing 1978), pp. 21–22.

21. One example of such interpreted meaning is illocutionary force in speech-act analysis (a concept which has been used by Beardsley, among others, in attempts to define literary discourse). Apropos of what he sees as Fish's identification of illocutionary force and meaning in general, Reichert points out that "in a situation in which the sentences 'I have to tie my shoes,' 'I have to eat popcorn,' and 'I hate movies' would all be understood as rejections of an invitation to the movies, no one would mistake the meaning of one for that of either of the other two" (p. 168). Reichert seems to point out the distinction (ignored by Fish) between what Frege calls "meaning" and "reference," that is, between meaning and the assumption of semantic equivalence (or reference) which Wimsatt suggests is constitutive of ordinary discourse.

22. There is no reason in theory why either of these meanings would have to be "literal" for this situation to obtain. In fact, not only is Ophelia's description of Hamlet as a rose not "literal" (as I will argue shortly), but neither is the "real" meaning of that description, which has to do with Hamlet's being the heir apparent, since Hamlet is himself a figure for a meaning at a higher level.

Fish would be right to insist (as he does in similar cases) that "Hamlet's position as heir apparent" (or something like that) has the better claim to "literalness" over "rose," since it is presumably the information about Hamlet and not information about a flower which is, at this level, Shakespeare's message. But reversing an opposition is not the same as eliminating it. We are still left with a nonliteral meaning, in addition to what Fish sees as the "literal" one. In reducing metaphor (and other literary oppositions) to a similar term (the tenor or message), Fish eliminates perhaps exactly that which makes such messages literary. Cf. also Reichert's defense of Searle's notion of the "indirect speech act" as "one that is performed *by means of* a direct speech act" (p. 167).

23. This tendency characterizes even Fish's most recent work. In the Fish/Iser debate waged recently in *Diacritics* (11 and 13 [1981]), one is sympathetic to Fish's criticism of Iser's insistence that *something* (however unknowable it might be) precedes the act of interpretation. But Fish's insistence that *nothing* precedes the act of interpretation is no less dogmatic and also shows a lingering objectivism. Both men seem to overlook a point I have tried to argue, namely that the structure of "what is given" and "what is supplied" is not at all dependent on the absolute objectivity of the former.

24. Cf. Ray, pp. 65–66.

25. Fish suggests this possibility himself in his many references to what he calls the "standard story" (e.g., pp. 199, 239). Fish's "new" definition of "literature" is, furthermore, not incompatible with the view I am describing here: literature is, says Fish, "language around which we have drawn a frame, a frame that indicates a decision to regard with a particular self-consciousness

the resources language has always possessed" (pp. 108–109). Forgetting these resources is, I have suggested, constitutive of "ordinary" discourse.

26. But somewhere, beyond Space and Time,
    Is wetter water, slimier slime!
    And there (they trust) there swimmeth One,
    Who swam ere rivers were begun. . . .
    And in that Heaven of all their wish,
    There shall be no more land, say fish.
    (1915)

Chapter Four

1. See *Ways of Worldmaking*, pp. 57–70.

2. Paul de Man, *Blindness and Insight: Essays in the Rhetoric of Contemporary Criticism* (New York: Oxford Univ. Press, 1971), p. 24.

3. I do not mean to suggest that these categories exist in a pure form: even in "ordinary" discourse, it is unlikely that the message itself could ever be absolutely neutral or, conversely, that in literature the speaker's intention could ever be absolutely irrelevant.

4. Cf. Roman Jakobson, "Closing Statement: Linguistics and Poetics," in *Style in Language*, ed. Thomas A. Sebeok (Cambridge: MIT Press, 1960), pp. 350–77. Although Jakobson associates the "poetic" function of language with an emphasis on the message itself, he discusses the "palpability of signs" (p. 356) in terms of sound patterns, diction, and syntax. Wimsatt's notion of "dramatic" utterance allows for an entirely semantic understanding of self-referentiality in literature, and thus avoids the pitfalls of pure formalism.

5. "The Concept of Literature," in Frank Brady, John Palmer, and Martin Price, eds., *Literary Theory and Structure* (New Haven: Yale Univ. Press, 1973), p. 34.

6. "On Meaning and Reference," p. 62.

7. Franz Kafka, "Die Verwandlung," in *Gesammelte Schriften*, Band I (Berlin: Schocken Verlag, 1935), my translation.

8. Beardsley himself seems to be at a loss to explain why utterances in literature do not have their normal "illocutionary force": that its withdrawal is signaled by "formal" or "internal" features is a position he is "no longer convinced . . . can be maintained" ("The Concept of Literature," p. 35). In "Aesthetic Intentions and Fictive Illocutions," Beardsley proposes the following explanation: "Perhaps . . . in publishing a poem, the writer himself abstracts the original text from the occasion of utterance. . . . This second locutionary action (the act of issuing, as distinct from the act of writing) gives us no assurance that the writer has performed the purported illocutionary

actions, and thus grants us permission (invites us) to take the poem as a fiction." See Paul Hernadi, ed., *What is Literature?* (Bloomington: Indiana Univ. Press, 1978), p. 175. I am suggesting that this "second locutionary action" amounts to a kind of quotation; however, I do not think I have solved the problem of how the second locution secures uptake as an illocutionary act— namely, the act of quoting. Beardsley's claim that the suspension of normal illocutionary force is triggered by our recognition of an "aesthetic intention"—"the intention to make something capable of affording aesthetic satisfaction to one who properly approaches it" (p. 165)—is unsatisfactory in at least two ways. On the one hand, this idea seems dangerously close to the error Wimsatt and Beardsley labelled the "intentional fallacy." However, when Beardsley tries to argue that the "aesthetic intention" is signaled internally by fictiveness (p. 175) and "semantic density, or multiplicity of meanings" (p. 176), he argues in a circle, because, by his own claim, the "aesthetic intention" must be signaled before those literary qualities can be recognized. To my mind the best solution so far is that of Wolfgang Iser, who claims that the literary force of a discourse is triggered by strategic gaps or deviations which frustrate the discourse's normal meaning. See *The Act of Reading*, especially chapter 4, part B, sections 2 and 3.

9. Cf. Barbara Herrnstein Smith: "I wish to propose that . . . the fictive representation of discourse . . . is precisely what defines that class of verbal compositions we have so much trouble naming and distinguishing, i.e., 'imaginative literature' or 'poetry in the broad sense'" (p. 140). Similar notions have also been advanced by Richard Ohmann, "Speech Acts and the Definition of Literature," *Philosophy and Rhetoric* 4 (Winter, 1971), pp. 1–19 and John R. Searle, *Speech Acts: An Essay in the Philosophy of Language* (London: Cambridge Univ. Press, 1969), pp. 78–79.

10. In suggesting that Wimsatt's notion of the "verbal icon" can be understood in terms of self-referentiality, I should once again emphasize that the sort of self-referentiality I have in mind is more Fregean (semantically-oriented) than Jakobsonean (formalist). Since the salt shaker in the preceding paragraph could be said to express the laws of physics, it might be objected that all natural events function iconically. To the extent that a natural event is taken as a *reference to* a law of physics, it would not function iconically to be sure. But the "meaning" of a natural event would be foregrounded to the extent that it is taken as what Nelson Goodman calls a "sample" or "exemplification" of such a law, that is, as symbolizing qualities that the event or symbol actually has, just as often occurs in the theater (for example, in the case of any prop). Cf. *Ways of Worldmaking*, pp. 32, 65–68.

11. The idea that "double," "multiple," or "dual" meaning *(référence dédoublée)* is characteristic of literary or symbolic discourse has been set forth by Paul Ricoeur, "The Problem of Double Meaning as Hermeneutic Problem

and as Semantic Problem," in *The Conflict of Interpretations* (Evanston: North-western Univ. Press, 1974), pp. 63 ff. Originally published as *Le Conflit des interprétations: Essais d'herméneutique* (Paris: Editions du Seuil, 1969).

12. See note 6.

13. More "abstract," as Wimsatt says, *The Verbal Icon*, p. xviii.

GLOSSARY

Interpretive Fallacy: The act of imputing meaning to a text on the basis of external evidence about the author's intention is a special case of the act of imputing meaning to a text on any basis whatsoever. Whenever explication (or "interpretation") purports to give us the meaning of a particular text, it is necessarily limited to giving us the meaning (or more properly the "reference") of the explication. In a sense, "reference" is always the imputing of something (specifically, a truth-value) to "meaning."

Intention: The *Encyclopedia of Philosophy* lists four basic uses of the word: (1) expressions of intention, (2) ascriptions of intention, (3) descriptions of the intention with which some action is done, and (4) classifications of actions as intentional or as done with intention. In the difference between intention and action in 1, 2, and 4 we see the logical distinction that forms the basis for the debate about authorial intention: the distinction between action planned and action accomplished (the action in this case being understood as meaning). However, the question becomes more complicated by the fact that one definition of meaning corresponds to sense 3 above. Consequently, it is useful to distinguish between the following different kinds of literary intention.

Active Intention (Michael Hancher): The achieved meaning of the text as a personal utterance for the author. As Hancher uses the term, it conflates the author's programmatic intention (see) with the text's operative intention (see) as the author understands it. If we disentangle what is new in this concept, we are left with a special case of operative intention. However, there are two complications. First, an active intention is, by definition, *not* an operative intention, since, though it is the author's, it is being urged upon, rather than independently established by, the interpreter. Active intentions must therefore be ascribed and thus, if they are to be different from programmatic intentions, must at some point undergo a problematic transformation into operative intentions for the reader. (See "sharable intention.") The other complication is that active intention presupposes that the author is a reader of his or her own text. It is not immediately clear why the author may not be susceptible to the same uncertainty as other readers or why he or she does not lose "authorial" status when functioning as a reader. In any case, the establishment of an active intention, like that of a programmatic intention, is no more assured than it is that the ascription can be made operative.

Construed, Implied, or Ascriptive Intention: Suresh Raval argues that "a construal of intention is implied in an act of interpretation," a view shared by Hirsch and Juhl. The term "operative intention," since it is equivalent to "achieved meaning" (see), would seem to cover this sense also. The difference is that Raval, Hirsch, and Juhl, unlike Wimsatt and Beardsley, would deny that there could be such a thing as an achieved meaning that was *not* an operative intention.

Determinant Intention: If meaning is understood *as* intent, that is, as someone's intention in making an utterance (see sense 3 under **Intention**) then the author's programmatic intention, once it is established, counts ipso facto as the utterance's operative intention. Determinant intentions are accepted by Wimsatt and Beardsley, but only as operative in ordinary discourse; indeed, it is their contention that literary discourse is distinct precisely because this principle of determinacy is suspended. On the other hand, Hirsch and, to an even greater extent, Peter D. Juhl feel that this principle holds in literary discourse as well.

Operative Intention (Wimsatt and Beardsley):   The achieved meaning of the text, such that, by its very existence, it is evidence of a programmatic intention (see). However, the status of an operative intention is in no way dependent on its validity as evidence; even if it is shown flatly to contradict the author's stated or inferred plan, it is still in some sense the effectuation of some plan, insofar as a programmatic intention may be construed from it.

Programmatic Intention (Michael Hancher):   The author's plan to mean something or the meaning he planned to put into effect. Expressions of intention (sense 1 under **Intention**) would serve as evidence, no more or less, for programmatic intentions; ascriptions of intention would be the corresponding act for an interpreter, with the same limitations. Programmatic intentions, even once established beyond a doubt, might correspond to the meaning of the text, but, whether or not they did, the two should be understood to function independently, such that neither could be offered as conclusive evidence of the other.

Sharable Intention (E. D. Hirsch):   The operative intention for the author understood as capable of being transformed (without being deformed) into the operative intention for a reader. Sharable intentions seem identical to active intentions (as Hancher understands them) and are problematic in the same way.

Meaning: When Wimsatt and Beardsley speak of achieved, accomplished, or operative meaning, they seem to have in mind any effective meaning whatsoever, as opposed to meaning that is merely imputed. This distinction is deceptive, however, because it presupposes a mode of meaning that is not imputed, that is, nonascriptive. For Wimsatt and Beardsley, this is characteristic of literary meaning, ordinary meaning being ascriptive. For others (Hirsch and Juhl), all meaning is ascriptive; hence, Wimsatt and Beardsley's distinction does not hold. It is useful, then, to distinguish between the following uses of the term "meaning."

"Meaning" (Frege, Hirsch):   The primary cognitive force of an utterance which is peculiar to that utterance. Needless to say, what is usually understood by the term meaning is closer to Frege's "reference" than to his "meaning." Critics often speak of "what a text means" and mean thereby another utterance to which the one being explicated is equivalent. One implication of Frege's distinction between "meaning" and "reference" is that much of what is referred to as *meaning* is not actually "meaning" at all. After Frege's concept of "meaning" is introduced in chapter two, "meaning" (in quotes) always indicates that concept unless otherwise specified. When the word *meaning* (without quotes) occurs, I usually wish to allude to the common literary-critical use of that term, generally for the purpose of demonstrating the contradiction which arises from that use.

Active Meaning, Operative Meaning, Accomplished Meaning, Effective Meaning: Nonpartisan terms which refer to a reader's actual understanding of an utterance, whether that understanding is ascriptive or nonascriptive.

Ascriptive Meaning, Imputed Meaning: The active meaning of a text, constituted by the determination of the author's programmatic or active intention (my terms to describe the theory of meaning challenged by Wimsatt and Beardsley).

Author's Meaning, Sharable Meaning (Hirsch): The active meaning of a text for its author (as reader), understood as accessible to another reader.

Dual Meaning (Paul Ricoeur): "By this I designate a certain meaning effect, according to which one expression, of variable dimensions, while signifying one thing at the same time signifies *another* thing *without ceasing to signify the first*" (p. 63, second emphasis mine). I emphasize the final prepositional phrase to make clear that "dual meaning" is neither a) the substitution of one meaning for another, nor b) simple ambiguity (i.e., multiplicity of meaning), but rather a structural relationship. The concept of "dual meaning" has certain affinities with Frege's notion of "indirect discourse" and Goodman's notion of "exemplification." For both Ricoeur and Goodman, this structural relation is characteristic of symbolic language (i.e., of literary discourse, conceived broadly).

Perceptual Meaning: 1) The intentional unity emerging from a perceptual multiplicity (Husserl: "intention is the meaning of perception"); 2) (Hirsch) The sharable, stable object, along the lines of Husserl's perceptual model, of a verbal utterance or a multiplicity of verbal utterances.

Textual Meaning (Beardsley): The active meaning of a text, where the text is understood as the best evidence of (if not actually identical to) its meaning, and where that meaning is logically prior to inferences about authorial intention of any kind.

Reference (Frege): A use which is made of "meaning" whenever it is submitted to a judgment of its truth-value with regard to its correspondence to a referent (see). When "meaning" is taken as meaning in the general and rather vague sense, it is taken as a kind of "reference," and the result is a loss of semantic individuality. The utterance in question then becomes operative at a level at which it is identical to an indefinite number of other "meanings." Put another way, when we "refer," we are not concerned with "meaning" but with truth-value.

Referent: That to which we can use "meaning" to refer. The ontological status of the referent is open to philosophical debate, the outcome of which does not affect my argument in any significant way. I would say that, whenever we speak of such-and-such as the "referent" of an utterance, we fill in the "such-and-such" with what is simply another utterance. What happens in such cases is not so much that a "referent" is supplied as that a "reference" is assumed (as the basis of the two utterances' equivalence). Such a case is exemplified in literary explication.

Semantic: Pertaining to meaning. When I say that the notion of literary meaning presupposed by the doctrine of the intentional fallacy is semantic rather than purely formal, I have in mind the fact that the entire debate about authorial intention needs to be rethought in terms of the distinction between "meaning" and "reference" rather than that between form and meaning (in the sense of content).

Semantic Autonomy (Hirsch): The notion that the literary text is independent of context or explanatory information, specifically, knowledge of the author's intention. Hirsch uses this term to characterize what he feels is the popular version of the notion of the "intentional fallacy" (see *Validity in Interpretation*, pp. 1 ff. and 10 ff.). My point is that, even though meaning does take place within a context, descriptions of context cannot be equated with and substituted for meaning.

Semantic Equivalence: Wimsatt suggests that the difference between poetic and practical (or ordinary) meaning is related to the fact that, in the former case, "no two different words or different phrases ever mean fully the same" whereas, in the latter case, they "can and do mean the same" (*The Verbal Icon*, pp. xii–xiii). I call the situation characteristic of nonpoetic discourse—or, as Goodman might say, "*when* literature is *not*"—"semantic equivalence." Note that the assumption that two or more utterances have the same "reference" (and hence their practical identity) is in no way dependent either upon the real existence of the referent or the true synonymy of their meanings.

Significance (Hirsch): The relation of "meaning" to "anything whatsoever." Since Frege's concept of "reference" does presuppose a fully realized "meaning," which is then related to a truth-value (and to other "equivalent" meanings), there is some validity to Hirsch's adoption of the concept in his argument concerning "significance."

BIBLIOGRAPHY

Aune, Bruce. "Intention." *Encyclopedia of Philosophy.* Vol. 4 (1967).

Beardsley, Monroe C. "Aesthetic Intentions and Fictive Illocutions." In Hernadi, Paul, ed. *What Is Literature?* Bloomington: Indiana University Press, 1978.

―――. *Aesthetics: Problems in the Philosophy of Criticism.* New York: Harcourt, Brace, and World, 1958.

―――. "The Concept of Literature." In Brady, Frank; John Palmer; and Martin Price, eds. *Literary Theory and Structure.* New Haven: Yale University Press, 1973.

―――. *The Possibility of Criticism.* Detroit: Wayne State University Press, 1970.

―――. "Textual Meaning and Authorial Meaning." *A Symposium on E. D. Hirsch's* Validity in Interpretation. *Genre* 3 (1968). *Symposium,* 174–77.

Black, Max, and Peter Geach, eds. *Translations from the Philosophical Writings of Gottlob Frege.* Oxford: Basil Blackwell, 1952.

Boeckh, August. *Enzyklopädie und Methodologie der philologischen Wissenschaften.* Leipzig: Teubner Verlag, 1886.

Booth, Wayne. *The Rhetoric of Fiction.* Chicago: University of Chicago Press, 1961.

De Man, Paul. *Blindness and Insight: Essays in the Rhetoric of Contemporary Criticism.* New York: Oxford University Press, 1971.

Demetz, Peter; Thomas Greene; and Lowry Nelson, Jr. *The Disciplines of Criticism*. New Haven: Yale University Press, 1968.

Fish, Stanley. *Is There a Text in This Class?* Cambridge: Harvard University Press, 1980.

—. "Why No One's Afraid of Wolfgang Iser." *Diacritics* 11, No. 2 (1981).

Frege, Gottlob. "Über Sinn and Bedeutung." In Black, Max, and Peter Geach, eds. *Translations from the Philosophical Writings of Gottlob Frege*. Oxford: Basil Blackwell, 1952.

Gadamer, Hans Georg. *Truth and Method*. New York: Seabury Press, 1975.

—. *Wahrheit und Methode*. Tübingen, W. Germany: Mohr, 1960.

Goodman, Nelson. *Ways of Worldmaking*. Indianapolis: Hackett Publishing, 1978.

Hancher, Michael. "The Science of Interpretation and the Art of Interpretation." *Modern Language Notes* 85 (1970), 795–97.

—. "Three Kinds of Intention." *Modern Language Notes* 87 (1972).

Hirsch, E. D. *The Aims of Interpretation*. Chicago: University of Chicago Press, 1976.

—. *Innocence and Experience: An Introduction to Blake*. New Haven: Yale University Press, 1964.

—. *Validity in Interpretation*. New Haven: Yale University Press, 1967.

Holland, Norman. "Stanley Fish, Stanley Fish." *Genre* 10, No. 3 (1977).

Hoy, David. *The Critical Circle: Literature, History, and Philosophical Hermeneutics*. Berkeley: University of California Press, 1978.

Hume, Robert D. "Intention and the Intrinsic in Literature." *College English* 29 (1967–68).

Huntley, John. "A Practical Look at E. D. Hirsch's *Validity in Interpretation.*" *Symposium*, 242–55.

Husserl, Edmund. *Cartesianische Meditationen.* Vol. I of *Husserliana.* The Hague: Martinus Nijhof, 1950.

————. *Ideen zu einer reinen Phänomenologie und phänomenologische Philosophie*, Book One. Halle/Saale : Max Niemeyer, 1913.

————. *Ideas.* Trans. W. R. Boyce Gibson. New York: Humanities Press, 1931.

————. *Cartesian Meditations.* Trans. Dorion Cairns. The Hague: Martinus Nijhof, 1977.

Isenberg, Arnold. "Some Problems of Interpretation." In Wright, Arthur F., ed. *Studies in Chinese Thought.* Chicago: University of Chicago Press, 1953.

Iser, Wolfgang. *The Act of Reading: A Theory of Aesthetic Response.* Baltimore: Johns Hopkins University Press, 1978.

————. *Der Akt des Lesens.* Munich: W. Fink Verlag, 1976.

————. *The Implied Reader.* Baltimore: Johns Hopkins University Press, 1974.

————. *Der implizite Leser.* Munich: W. Fink, 1972.

————. "Talking Like Whales." *Diacritics* 11, No. 3 (1981).

Jakobson, Roman. "Closing Statement: Linguistics and Poetics." In Thomas A. Sebeok, ed. *Style in Language.* Cambridge: MIT Press, 1960, 350–377.

Josipovici, Gabriel, ed. *The Modern English Novel: The Reader, The Writer, and the Work.* New York: Harper and Row, 1976.

Juhl, Peter D. "Intention and Literary Interpretation." *Deutsche Vierteljahrsschrift für Literaturwissenschaft und Geistesgeschichte* 13, No. 3 (1973).

——. *Interpretation: An Essay in the Philosophy of Literary Criticism.* Princeton: Princeton University Press, 1980.

Kafka, Franz. "Die Verwandlung." *Gesammelte Schriften*, Vol. I. Berlin: Schocken Verlag, 1935.

Kintgen, Eugene R. "Effective Stylistics." *Centrum* 2, No. 1 (1975).

Kupperman, Joel J. "Art and Aesthetic Experience." *The British Journal of Aesthetics* 15 (1975).

Lane, Jeremy. "His Master's Voice? The Questioning of Authority in Literature." *The Modern English Novel: The Reader, The Writer, and the Work.* Gabriel Josipovici, ed. New York: Harper and Row, 1976.

Loewenberg, Ina. "Intentions: The Speaker and the Artist." *The British Journal of Aesthetics* 15 (1975).

MacLeish, Archibald. *Collected Poems 1917–1952.* Boston: Houghton Mifflin, 1952.

Maier, Rosemarie. "The 'Intentional Fallacy' and the Logic of Literary Criticism." *College English* 32, No. 2 (1970–71).

Marshall, Donald G. Review of E. D. Hirsch, *The Aims of Interpretation. Philosophical Quarterly* 56 (1977), 52–55.

Miller, J. Hillis. "The Geneva School" *The Critical Quarterly* 8, No. 4 (1966), 305–21.

Mohanty, J. N. "Husserl and Frege: A New Look at Their Relationship." *Research in Phenomenology* 4 (1974).

Mueller-Vollmer, Kurt. "To Understand an Author Better Than the Author Himself: On the Hermeneutics of the Unspoken." *Language and Style* 5, No. 1 (1971), 43–52.

Nietzsche, Friedrich. "Über Wahrheit and Lüge im aussermoralischen Sinne." *Friedrich Nietzsche: Werke in drei Bänden*, Vol. III. Munich: Carl Hanser Verlag, 1966.

Ohmann, Richard. "Speech Acts and the Definition of Literature." *Philosophy and Rhetoric* 4 (1971), 1–19.

Olsen, Stein Haugom. "Authorial Intention." *The British Journal of Aesthetics* 45 (1971).

Peckham, Morse. "The Intentional? Fallacy?" *New Orleans Review* 1 (1968–69), 124.

Quine, Willard. "A Postscript on Metaphor." *Critical Inquiry* 5 (1978–79), 161–62.

Rader, Ralph. "Explaining Our Literary Understanding: A Response to Jay Schleusener and Stanley Fish." *Critical Inquiry* 1, No. 4 (1975).

Ray, William. "Supersession and the Subject: A Reconsideration of Stanley Fish's 'Affective Stylistics'." *Diacritics* 8 (1978).

Reichert, John. "But That Was in Another Ball Park: A Reply to Stanley Fish." *Critical Inquiry* 6, No. 1 (1979).

Ricoeur, Paul. *Le Conflit des interprétations: Essais d'herméneutique.* Paris: Editions du Seuil, 1969.

————. "The Problem of Double Meaning as Hermeneutic Problem and as Semantic Problem." *The Conflict of Interpretations*. Evanston, Ill.: Northwestern University Press, 1974.

Searle, John R. *Speech Acts: An Essay in the Philosophy of Language.* London: Cambridge University Press, 1969.

Sebeok, Thomas A., ed. *Style in Language.* Cambridge: MIT Press, 1960.

Seidler, Ingo. "The Iconolatric Fallacy: On the Limitations of the Internal Method of Criticism." *The Journal of Aesthetics and Art Criticism* 26 (1967).

Shipley, Joseph T., ed. *Dictionary of World Literature*. New York: Philosophical Library, 1942.

Smith, Barbara Herrnstein. *On the Margins of Discourse*. Chicago: University of Chicago Press, 1978.

Steig, Michael. "The Intentional Phallus: Determining Verbal Meaning in Literature." *The Journal of Aesthetics and Art Criticism* 36 (1977), 52–55.

Strawson, Peter F. "On Referring." *Mind* 59 (1950), 320–44.

Wellek, René and Austin Warren. *Theory of Literature*. New York: Harcourt, Brace, 1949.

Wimsatt, W. K. "Genesis: An Argument Resumed." *Day of the Leopards*. New Haven: Yale University Press, 1976.

———. *The Verbal Icon*. Lexington: University of Kentucky Press, 1954.

Wittgenstein, Ludwig. *Philosophische Untersuchungen* (I, 23). Trans. (with German text) by G. E. M. Anscombe. Oxford: Basil Blackwell, 1953.